Real Talk Media

Presents

Two For Five

A Novel

Lawrence D. Brown

Email: lawrencedbrown245@yahoo.com
Available online
https://www.createspace.com/4274969

Copyright © 2009 by Darryl Brown

ISBN: 978-0-615-30689-6

Street Level Publications
P.O Box 311135
Jamaica, NY 11431

Cover Design: ArtBookbindery.com
Editor: Louise Brown
Typeset: Linda Williams

Printed and bound in the United States Of America

Dedication

I dedicate this book to my family. Thank God for all of you. I give thanks to my Moms for all her prayers. To my sister, for keeping your foot in my tail, my lady for all her support and lastly, a special thanks to my kids, Rashid, Shaquille, Ketric and Zamara. You need to know I love you all and need you guys in my life.

This book is for you....

CRITIC REVIEWS

Intense and Captivating....
This book is good!!! Couldn't put it down....Very well written....As you read *TWO FOR FIVE* you will be drawn into the events....Congratulations to author Lawrence D. Brown for a very impressive debut....***Barbara Morgan***

Gripping
TWO FOR FIVE is an absolute page-turner.... I loved it....The author wrote it from personal experience....Great read with a positive message....
Diamonds Literary World

Great read!!!

This book was a great read, with a positive message...you'll go through a multitude of emotions reading this book. I encourage young men and women to read this! **--Ms. Stephie Baby**

Thank you Lawrence D. Brown for allowing me to read your story ;) --
DIVAS & GENTS INTO URBAN/STREET LIT!

BLAST FROM THE PAST
I loved this book....I recommend it to friends, book clubs and avid readers.
Deja Vu Book Club

Chapter One

Eleven O'clock, I'm just getting up. Nothing like a good nights sleep. I feel good this morning. I should. Yesterday, my black ass was waking up to the sounds of prison guards yelling, "five minutes 'til chow." Gothen Annex, that's the name of the prison I was in. I spent four years there. Yesterday I was released. Gothen Annex is a maximum correctional facility for juveniles in Upstate New York. From the age of sixteen 'til I was twenty-one, I'd been waking up to the same bullshit. I flung the covers off me, sat on the edge of my bed and smiled as the sun shined through my bedroom window. I could feel the warmth of the sun's heat. Thinking back to when I was away, the sun never felt, or even shined, through the small window of my cell, as it did this morning. Up there, even in the summer, it felt like winter. Anyway, I got out of bed, washed up, got dressed and went downstairs. Nobody's home. My Moms must've gone to work. It's been four years since I had the entire house to myself. My family lives in Laurelton, Queens. Nice middle class neighborhood. On the living room table, I found a note my moms left. It read:

> "Good morning Niko, glad you're home, and hope you slept well. I didn't want to wake you but I had to go to work. The twenty dollars you found with this letter I thought might come in handy. I made your favorite, home fries and beef sausage. You'll find the plate covered on the stove. Call me later if you need to. Welcome home!"
>
> Love Mom

Thank God for Moms. The aroma of my first home cooked meal in years, filled my nose, and lead me straight to the source. I was about to take a healthy spoon full, when I heard a car horn. I walked to the front window, still holding the plate of course, and opened the front door.

I stepped out on to the front steps. Once again, the sun's rays felt different. At that moment, I absolutely knew I was home. I didn't have to ask a C.O. to open my cell. My boys pulled up in what looked to be a brand new car, the sun reflected off its shiny exterior. When I was locked down, my boys made sure I didn't want for nothing. They even made sure my family was alright. My next-door neighbors, Mr. and Mrs. Jenkins, came out of their house.

Niko, when you get home, Ms. Jenkins asked?

Yesterday, I replied.

How you doing?

Fine Ms. Jenkins.

Why didn't you come by to let me know you were home?

I apologize, Ms. Jenkins, I'll see you later on when you come home from work.

Her husband remarked, good to see you back. Make sure you come by later, okay?

Yes sir, I said respectfully.

They waved good-bye, got in their car and pulled off. Mr. and Mrs. Jenkins have been my neighbors for as long as I've been on this earth. Good people. They've known my family since we moved in the neighborhood back when I was a baby. When I got locked up, my mother was twisted behind that shit. They helped her deal with the fact that her baby boy was taken away from her. Now that I look back on things, I was outta control. My mother would've had a nervous breakdown had it not been for the Jenkins. As I said, my boys pulled up in front of the house in a brand new ride. I walked to the car, opened the back door and clouds of smoke escaped.

"What up Niko," Chase asked?

"Ain't nothin' kid. How you?"

"I'm good," he quickly responds.

Chase and I have known each other since Elementary School. He's the pretty boy type. Always chasing the girls. That's why we named him "Chase". Ming, on the other hand, is business minded like me, but one things absolutely for sure he ain't a morning person. If I remember correctly, he usually didn't get up 'til noon. His brain doesn't seem to function right 'til 12:01. But he's loyal, and very protective of the ones he's closest to, like Chase and I. Ming and I go back like eight track players. We grew up together from when we were in pampers. My sister baby-sat for his moms, who lived two doors down from my house. Ever since then, we've been running hard. Today's important, that's why he's up so early. We slap each other five. The smoke from the spliff they're puffin' surrounds me.

"You need some air back there," Chase asked.

"Yeah kid, y'all got the car lit."

I could see Ming's bloodshot eyes through the rear view mirror. Chase turned around to see if I had enough legroom. I could tell the weed had them lifted cause their eyes had that chinky look. Ming turned up the music on the radio. Evelyn Champagne King was singing her hit single, "You make my love come down". She did her thing on that record. The bass from the music had the car vibrating. We pulled off, turned the corner, and ran into a red light. A car pulled up next to us. Their music played just as loud. We looked over at them. They looked back as us. Three women sat patiently for the light to turn green. They smiled. We smiled back. As the light changed, they waved goodbye.

Chase told Ming, "catch up to them so I can holla at 'em."

Ming stepped on the gas. The engine revved up and the car took flight. Our cars glided side by side up the boulevard. Chase rolls down his window and waits for the driver to do the same.

"Pull over," Chase yells.

"We can't right now, we're runnin' late," the lady responds.

"Late for what," Chase asked.

"Why," she questions.

"I wanna talk to you for a sec. Maybe we can go somewhere and have lunch or something, get to know one another.

We came to a red light.

She asks Chase, "do you have a number?"

Chase turned around, winked at me, and said "got one."

Finding a pen, he wrote his number down and tries to pass it to her as the two cars stood still. The light turns green. They pull off before he has a chance to pass his number. Ming slams on the gas to catch them. Three lights pass. We catch up to them at the corner of Merrick and Linden. Chase rolls down his window again. The driver rolls hers down. Chase asked, "what's your name?"

She says, "Lisa."

"I'm Chase."

She smiles and said sarcastically, "yeah, I can tell."

He leans out the window to pass her his number. She takes it, looks at it, and says, I'll call you, and rolls up her window. We turned off Merrick onto Foch Boulevard heading towards the Van Wyke Expressway.

"What's up y'all, where we headin'," I asked.

No one responds.

I asked again. "Where we goin' Ming?"

"We got some business to take care of," he replies. "I told everybody to meet us at the shop." "Who's everybody?"

"The whole crew, you'll see when we get there. We got some changes to make," Ming commented. "What kind of changes," I asked.

"Big things bout to happen," Chase interjects.

We roll up to the shop. People were hanging out front, cars were pulling up behind us, and inside, the place was packed. People were getting haircuts, but mostly, all "the crew" gathered.

"Today's Friday. Pay day," Chase said. "Naturally, everybody's here." As we walked in, the talking seemed to dull down. People walked up to Ming and Chase giving them handshakes, and looking at me suspiciously saying "who's this?" Some I knew, others Ming introduced me to. "This my man Niko, you'll find out who he is in a minute."

"Alright, alright, let's get this shit started," Ming yelled.

Ming stood in the back of the shop facing everybody. Behind him, a big screen TV showed the BET channel. Some sat in barber chairs, others stood where they could. Ming began by saying; "some of you already know my man Niko. He's been locked down for the last four years. He came home yesterday, and I'm glad he's back. It's because of him, that we got shit poppin' like we do. He's the one that put Chase and me on to slingin' out here. Doin' that hand to hand shit. We sold weed for him by Key Food on Merrick back in the day. As y'all know, we ain't stop there.

After he got knocked, we stepped up our game by slingin' that hard shit. Now he's home, and we wanna give him his props, and put him on to getting this money with us. He's on paper right now with parole. He got about a year or so to give them mafuckas'. That's aight, cause Chase and me gotta spot for him right here at the shop." Ming looks at me and said, "we need you to come run with us. From the time you and I could crawl, we been runnin' together. I don't see why that should change now. Chase and I decided, for now, you could run both the barbershops and the Laundromat over in Hollis. Just to get you started. We ain't gonna let you go out like a sucka and be flippin' burgers at McDonalds or some shit. That ain't happenin'. As time goes on, we'll put you on to other things. But for now, hold that. We also ain't tryin' to have you too close to the street shit. At least not right now. What we want you to do is to handle the money." Ming raised his voice and yelled out so everybody could hear, "anybody gotta problem with dat?" Nobody responded. "You need to drop off cash, see Niko. You need to get paid, see Niko. Anything that has to do with who works where, he'll be the one to

7

speak to. All that shit, he got. Chase and me gonna concentrate on keepin' you brothers' on the street supplied with product. Before Niko got knocked, he was tellin' Chase and me a way we could increase our clientele. At first, I thought the idea was kinda crazy but, when I thought about it, it definitely made sense. Starting tonight, we gonna bring out something' new.

Two for five. Chase and me already got about five thousand dollars worth of product bagged up. What we gonna do is give out samples and let people test out product. Let 'em know we got the biggest and the best shit out. Anybody that ain't workin' with us, bout to be bounced out they spots.

Anytime we got product on the street, smokers need to be seeing us. No doubt. A mafucker got five dollars, we want it! Every fiend that smokes, every stunt that chokes, needs to know we got the biggest and the best shit out. The only time they go somewhere else, is when they can't find us. Which ain't gonna happen. Niko's bout to work out a schedule so everybody gets to eat. Instead of us being out there from three in the afternoon 'til whenever, we gonna be out there all day, all night. Straight twenty fours. We already know mafuckas' movin' they shit gonna have problems with how we roll, but guess what, fuck em'. We out here to get paid. Brothers' got problems with that, let 'em step up or shut up. We takin' slingin' to another level. Niko gonna be runnin' the shops, keepin' track of the cash, and he'll know at all times who's working where and when. Chase and me gonna handle keepin' niggas' in

8

check. Straight like that. We put together a crew that'll handle any problems we run into. You'll find out who they are when the time comes. Them bitch as niggas' that ran off with our shit, y'all know who I'm talkin' bout. Y'all even think about pulling that shit, you gonna have problems. For real."

I could hear brothers in the crowd mumblin', but nobody said anything. "Anyway, ma'fuckas' tappin' packs, stashin' cash on the low, or whatever else you niggas' be out there doin', that shit bout to be shut down. We find out you tappin' our shit, your ass gonna get got. You heard? This ain't no game.

Lets get that money. Ain't nothin' wrong with trickin' just don't let a bitch tap your pockets in the process. Otherwise, that shits on you. All you brother's that been holdin' down spots solo, don't worry, I got y'all. Y'all gonna be movin' up and having your own crew. Most importantly, remember, no more droppin' off cash to me or Chase, we hot right now.

Havin' the cops snatch our cash ain't gonna sit right with me. You need to drop off cash, see Niko. Only way Chase and me get involved, is if you got problems or need another pack. Niko's runnin' this shit, and we got his back. And just to let y'all know, don't think for a second you can play my man. The brother ain't soft or slow. Not by a long shot. As long as you handle your business, keep your count straight, and don't try no bullshit, the niggas' a good brother to have in your corner. No doubt! We already told him, anybody give you problems from this team, let us know, and we'll make an example of his ass. We already got a couple ma'fuckas in mind. Don't let it be you! Again, I strongly suggest not to sleep on my man. You'll fuck around and get stretched. You heard?"

As Ming spoke, I looked around the room to read people's facial expressions. I could tell off the bat, a few of these niggas gonna test me. No problem. They'll find out real quick, I ain't nobody to play with. Then it hit me, look how I'm thinking. Here I am just comin' home less than twenty-four hours ago, and already I'm back in this shit. I pulled Ming aside and walked him into an office in the back of the shop.

Listen man, I gotta really think about this shit y'all talkin' about. My P.O. already said, if I fuck up even slightly, she's sendin' my black ass back upstate on the first thing smokin'. That means I can't have nothin' to do with slingin'. Not right now. Nothin' - Ming interrupted me. Niko, Niko, don't worry, you aint' gonna be out there like that. As far as your

P.O. will know, you'll be working for a respectable business. There's no way anybody can trace shit back to me or Chase or anybody else for that matter.

All the businesses are registered under our Lawyer's name, and he ain't tellin' shit! We hit his ass off every month with a 'lil cash.

That ma'fuckas' good. Don't worry. We got this. That brings me to the next topic; you gonna need a car, cause we can't keep comin' to pick your ass up everyday. And besides, if you tryin' to keep shit legit looking for your bitch ass P.O. you need -"

"Ming, I need to talk to you." Shake, one of Ming's workers rushed in the office. "Pardon me, I didn't know you were busy." Nuh, go head, what's up?" "I just saw one of them kids that ran off with our work." "Where you see him at?" Ming asks? "By the store on Foch and 140th." "Go get that nigga, now! Bring his ass here." Shake rushed out the door. Ming yelled out to the other

workers in the front of the shop. "When Shake comes back, lock the front door, and nobody goes in or out. In fact stand outside, see if you see Shake anywhere. And keep an eye on the streets."

I turned to Ming and said, "if there's gonna be problems-" Ming interrupts me again and said, "you wanna leave?" He looked at me in disbelief that I would even fix my

mouth to say something like that. But I had to, cause I just came home and ain't trying to get caught up in no nonsense.

He went on to say, "I know Niko, I told you we don't want you too close to the bullshit. Not right now. And besides, we gotta protect out moneyman, right?"

I nodded my head in agreement. He called another one of our workers in the back room, and introduced me.

"Post, this is Niko. From now on, or until we get this nigga a car, you gonna be runnin' him round wherever he need to go. Understand?"

The brother shook his head in agreement. From the look in his eyes, I could tell he knew how serious Ming was. Ming and I continued to talk for about five or ten minutes. Shake came back, breathing heavy and told

Ming he didn't see the kid by the store but thought he might be at this crack spot over on 138th street. Ming hesitated for a second, I guess to figure out the best plan of action. Then he told Shake, "let's go." Ming snatched up his keys and jetted out the office. I sat behind the desk in the office thinking about the shit I'm about to get my ass in. Then I thought, this shit might work. Post came back in the office. He stood about six feet five, slender, brown skinned, with a big scar on the side of his face.

"You ready to go," he asked?

"Nah, I'm gonna wait a minute to see what jumps off. Just hang out in the front. I'll let you know when I'm ready."

"Aight. I'll be right out front."

As he walked out the office, I noticed his gun sticking out from under his shirt. I called him back in the office.

"If you gonna roll with me, I explained, you gotta keep shit on the low, kid. That means be aware of how you dress and carry yourself. We don't wanna draw no attention to us. Understand?"

"I guess you talkin' bout the gun on my side, right?"

"Yeah, cover that shit up."

As he pulled his shirt over his gun, he turned and walked out the office. I vaguely heard Ming in the front of the shop saying something about; "we'll catch that nigga some other time."

In any event, it looks like I'm back in this shit, win, lose or draw.

Chapter Two

It's been a month now since I came home. Everyday Post comes to pick me up and take me around to reacquaint me with the neighborhood. Post introduced me to all our workers, and showed me who's holding down what and where. Some of them I already know. I've been to all three stores Ming and Chase opened while I was gone. Both barbershops and the Laundromat are good fronts. I mentioned to Ming about opening a bar lounge. He said he was thinking the same thing. I had to report to my P.O. a couple of days ago. She wants me to go to this employment agency in Lower Manhattan to see if I can get a job working in a restaurant at the South Street Seaport. Same shit Ming said I'd be doing. Working in some hamburger joint flippin' burgers. I'm supposed to check that out on Monday. Later tonight I'm going out with Casandra to the movies and dinner. Things between she and I have been moving along well. Talking on the phone every night. Spending every moment we have, either at her house or mine. The other day, she told me she's been thinking about moving out of her mama's house and getting her own place. She asked me if I would come with her. I haven't given her an answer yet. More than likely I will. I like the fact she knows how to handle her business, and has a level head when it comes to dealing with things. She's been very supportive of me and lets me know on a regular how she feels about us being together. She even told me she wants to get married some day. When she said that, I looked at her for a minute, pointed to myself, and said, to me?

"Calm down, Casandra replied, I'm not talking about right now, but in a few years, when I finish college, I wanna make that move."

I can remember the look she had in her eyes when she said that, and the words she spoke as she looked in mine. I could feel how sincere and how serious she was.

"I wanna be with you, Niko, Casandra said passionately. I know if you and I put our heads together, we can do a lot for each other. We could have a beautiful life together, don't you think?"

Hell, I'm just coming home and this girl already got me married with kids. Truth is, I knew she was right. It's time I started thinking about holding down my own family, and she would be a good woman to do that with. I know she has a good head on her shoulders, being a junior in college and all. She's definitely not lazy. One thing's for sure, when she sees something she wants, she knows how to get it. That shows me she's focused and determined. Good qualities to have. I can also tell she's loyal. That's important, too. Without it, we ain't got nothin' but bullshit. She would definitely make someone a good wife. Why shouldn't it be me? I remember the day Casandra and I first met. It was a couple of days after I came home. I was sitting in my living room watching television flicking through the channels to find something to watch while I had breakfast. Something I hadn't been able to do in a long time. During the day, while I was locked down, I'd be working in the mess hall serving the prison population their meals and couldn't watch TV while I worked. I didn't know what to watch. Finally, I settled on some cartoons I found on one of the cable networks, and finished eating my breakfast. After I finished, I leaned back on the couch to smoke a cigarette. I thought about what I could do next. Should I mow the lawn or just chill out and relax? I damn sure ain't gonna sit here watching cartoons all day. Just then, someone knocked on the door.

I figured it was Post coming to pick me up. I went to the door, and peeked out the window. It was a girl. Gorgeous, I thought to myself. At first I didn't recognize her. Then slowly, it came to me. That looks like Casandra. She lives up the block from me. She and I had gone to junior high school together. When I opened the door, the first thing I noticed was her smile and her deep dimples. My eyes scanned her up and down. I still didn't recognize her completely, cause when we were in school together, she had a totally different look. She changed a lot. A hell of a lot. Her face was starting to become increasingly familiar. After being away, people change, and she most definitely did. I remember back in the day, when we went to school together, she wore these thick ass glasses and her face was covered with acne. She was thin as a rail and always had an arm full of books. Someone you *did not* want to be caught with. But damn, look at her now. When she spoke, her voice was soft and angelic. I stood there stuck in my tracks and admired her beauty. She had to call my name twice before I snapped out of my daze. She said sexily, "I'm glad to see you home," and gave me a hug and a kiss. As she slid her hand off my shoulder, I saw a flirtatious look in her eyes. I invited her in. She said she couldn't stay long, and just came by to welcome me home.

"How'd you know I was home," I asked?

She said, she was driving by with her mother the other day, and saw me outside with my friends. My questions continued.

"How'd you know I'd be home this morning?"

"I didn't. I just took a chance, rang the bell, and here I am. Beside I hadn't seen you in a while, and I wondered what had happened to you."

Good answer, I thought. I didn't remember speaking to her that much when we were in school. So, what's up with this? Is she feeling me? So I continued to ask questions.

Two For Five

"You said, you can't stay long, where you have to be?"

She said she had to be at work by eleven that morning. She worked at Macy's at the Green Acres Mall in Valley Stream. I walked her into the living room and allowed her to walk pass me so I could see what she was working with in the ass department. Especially since her hips looked as though she was holding. As she walked by, I complemented her on how sexy she looked. She had on a white T-Shirt that read, *Virginia is for Lovers*. Her shirt fit her loosely, but I could still see the size and shape of her breast. Just the thought of cupping them in my hands made my mouth water. The black pants she wore looked like leotards. I found out later, they're called stretch pants. The width of her hips and the bubble shape of her ass prevented her T-shirt from covering her shape. Allowing me to see every curve of her body. She looked back at me with that look she gave me earlier. She stood about five feet two, caramel complexion, long, straight, shoulder length, jet black hair, slightly bow legged with a pair of mesmerizing hazel eyes. We sat on the couch and talked about me being away. You know, what it was like, how long I was there, what did I do to keep busy, how did I keep from going crazy. Normal questions. As we talked, I found out that she had a crush on me since junior high. On that note, I slid a little closer, and watched her reaction. I took the opportunity to lean in close so that my face was about four or five inches away from hers. I whispered in a low masculine voice, "it's been a long time since I been this close to a beautiful woman."

I told her I appreciated her stopping by, and hoped that she and I could see more of each other in the future. She showed me that sexy smile again, exposing her perfectly polished teeth. I was impressed at how well she kept herself. You can always tell something about a person by the way they take care of their teeth. Out of nowhere, my thoughts shifted to one of those Colgate toothpaste commercials and I thought, she would make a damn good model. She brought me up to date with the things that had been going on in her life. Such as attending Queens Community College on Queens Boulevard, where she's studying Nursing. She said she has a B+ average so far, and a strong C in her Computer Networking course. I asked her if she had a boyfriend, she told me that she *had*, but he acted as though he didn't have time for her. I probed a little deeper, and found out that she, and whoever this guy was, hadn't been together in months, and that she wanted someone in her life that would show her the same care and concern she showed them. In my mind, I visualized raising my hand to volunteer for the position. I continued listening, attentively taking in the bits of information she was giving me and formulating an impression of her. The simple fact she was there, helped me realize she may be considering me to be that special someone in her life, and I was happy with her choice. No longer were my thoughts on making a move on her, at least not now. I could tell she wasn't that kind of girl. *Damn it!!* The best thing to do would be to allow things to flow naturally, and from where I was sitting, they seemed like they were. She asked me what I would be doing later, and if I was interested in going out somewhere, or maybe meeting her after work. I never met a girl who was so straightforward. It fascinated me. Hell, that shit turned me on. She noticed the time on the clock, and said she had to go.

I asked her if she didn't mind me riding with her to work. Her faced lit up. She smiled like she never had a man take her to work before. She said, "Yes," in that soft and angelic voice, "I'd like that." I returned the smile. Even though this was the first time she and I were *ever* this close, I felt like we definitely connected, and from the way she was responding to me, it seemed like she felt the same. I told her I had to go upstairs to get dressed. Before I stood up, I fastened the belt around my robe, trying to hide my rock hard jump off. When I stood up, she looked me up and down, as though she was trying to figure out which way to attack me. The look she had in her hazel eyes, and the way she held the tip of her finger between her slightly parted teeth, no words needed to be said. All the words we needed were said in the stares we exchanged. She stood up in front of me, and lifted her arms to place them around my neck. I moved closer to her, and wrapped my arms around her waist. Our bodies' snuggly pressed against each other. She immediately pushed her tongue down my throat. I fell back against the wall to support both our weights. Slowly guiding my hands down the small of her back until my pinky and ring fingers had slipped past the elastic band of her pants.

I could feel her tongue making circular motions around mine. Then she said in a sexy voice, "welcome home, Niko." She moaned as I massaged her shapely backside. She rubbed her leg tightly up and down mine. I held her thigh in one hand, and with the other, I cupped her ass. She could feel my erection throbbing against her inner thigh. I pulled my tongue from the grips of her mouth, and let her leg down slowly, looked her in the eyes, and told her, "come with me." Her hands slid from around my shoulders, and rested on my chest. She looked up at me and said, "lead the way Daddy." Again, she looked at the clock.

This time, she said let me call my job and tell 'em I'm gonna be late. I led her upstairs to my mom's room so she could use the phone. When she hung up, I picked her up off her feet, carried her into my room and laid her down softly on the bed. Our bodies pressed closely against each other, gyrating forcefully and passionately. I rose to my knees to pull my T-shirt off. She took off her clothes, and with the quickest of motions, she put me inside her. She let out a sigh of relief, letting me know, she was pleased.

Chapter Three

On my way back in the cab from dropping Casandra at work, I remembered Ming was coming over to the house to pick me up. I asked the driver to drive a little faster so I wouldn't miss him. When he turned the corner of my block, I saw a red BMW sitting in front my house. We pulled up along side. It was Ming. I paid the driver, got out the cab, and walked past Ming as he got out his car to sit on the hood. I told him to hold up a minute while I went inside to use the bathroom and get some money. When I came back he was sitting in the car. I opened the door and on the front seat were a pager, a pack of Newports, some rolling paper and a few other items. No sooner than I sat down, his pager started vibrating. He picked it up to see the number and mumbled something to himself I couldn't understand. I asked, is everything okay?

He said, in an uncertain tone, that everything was. "I just got a lot on my mind right now." "What's going on," I asked?

He looked at me real serious, and was about to say something when his pager went off again. This time he pulled over to use a payphone. I watched him as he spoke on the phone. I could tell he was angry by the gestures he was making with his hands. He slammed the phone down and walked back to the car, slamming the door behind him. As we pulled off he said, "we gotta make a couple of stops, aight?

"What's up," I asked?

His eyes focused on the road like he was in deep thought.

"Niko, you ever feel like sayin' fuck it sometime?"

"Yeah, I do, but I can't let shit flow like that. I asked him again.

What's goin' on? Everything cool? What's up?"

He pulled over to the side of the road and put the car in park. He started telling me what's on his mind.

"Niko, you just don't know man. I'm tryin' to keep my head together and get this money, but shits happening I don't like. I look out for niggas'. Put 'em on so they can get this money with us. Then the same niggas' turn around and steal from you. Shit's about to pop off. I just wanna do my thing and get paid. The kid I was looking for, you know, the one that ran off with our product, Chase just told me he found his ass. Where he at, I asked?

Chase said this head he knows was at this spot on 138th and Foch earlier today and saw 'em over there smokin'. I guess he's been hidin' out there since he ran off."

"How much was the pack you gave 'em," I asked?

"Fifteen hundred fuckin'dollars worth." Damn, that's fucked up and ain't nobody seen or heard from him 'til now?

So what you gonna do?

I could see the wheels turning in his head.

"Before we go over there, I gotta call my man Ras. He's this Jamaican kid from the Southside who's part of my "smash crew". He'll meet us over there. Chase gonna have that crack head bitch show us the house where that kid is. She'll knock on the door pretendin' she got something' for that nigga to smoke. As soon as the door opens, we'll push our way in. This nigga gonna be the one we use to send a message to everybody else. You don't fuckin' steal from us," Ming said intently. Chase met us on the corner of 138th and Foch with this smoked out lookin'chick.

Not long after, Ras showed up. Chase told the girl to knock on the door while we waited in the cut. I could hear someone inside ask, who is it? It was a man's voice. It's Jackie, the girl said, open the door, I got somethin'."

Once we heard the locks unlatch, and the door open slightly, Ras pushed the door open with his shoulder. Me, Chase and Ming rushed in behind him and slammed the door shut. I noticed the look on this niggas' face when he saw it was us. His mouth dropped open and his eyes got real wide. If that nigga could run, he'd probably be in Mexico some fuckin' where.

"What up Waters," Ming asked? "Where's my shit," he asked sternly? Waters started to open his mouth, but Ras slapped the shit out of him leaving his handprint on the side of his face. Blood oozed down his chin. You could hear the echo from the slap throughout the house. Ras snatched him off the floor with one hand and pinned him against the wall by his neck. His feet dangled about three feet off the ground. We heard footsteps coming down the stairs. Ras let Waters down, but still had him pinned against the wall and pulled out a big ass .45 automatic and stuck it in Waters' mouth. He gagged as Ras pushed it down his throat. I looked down to the floor as a puddle of piss rolled towards me. Waters' pissed himself. Whoever was coming down the stairs was trying to creep up on us. Ming pulled out his .380 and positioned himself behind the wall while pointing his gun to where he thought a person's head would be. I could hear the footsteps getting closer. Ming popped out from behind the wall and fired three shots. He missed. It was a little girl. She peaked around the wall where her father was hemmed up and started screaming.

"Leave my daddy alone, leave 'em, stop hittin' 'em, leave 'em alone," the little girl kept yelling.

Waters tried to say something but couldn't cause Ras still had that big ass .45 stuck in his mouth. Waters' little girl must've said that shit about twenty times before Ras took the gun out of his mouth. Waters told her to be quiet and go upstairs.

"Everything's okay, baby. Daddy'll be up in a minute to tuck you in."

"No," the little girl said defiantly. I ain't goin' nowhere."

Waters looked at her, wiped the blood from his face and said, "get your ass upstairs, *NOW!*" She backed away, wiping the tears from her eyes with her hand. We moved into the living room and saw on the table five stems, two packs of Newports, four lighters and a bunch of empty crack vials. The same vials Ming used to bag his shit.

"I see you been havin' a party," Ming commented. "I was gonna call you Ming, but -"

Ras smacked Waters in the mouth with the butt of the gun, knocking him to his knees. Blood gushed from his lips.

He lowered his hands from his mouth to show his two front teeth had been knocked out. Waters spit them on the floor.

"Stop fuckin" bloodclot lyin," Ras said with a deep Jamaican accent. You know you wasn't gonna call nobody. Where's the rest of our shit? Huh, where is it?"

Before he could answer, Ras hit him again with the butt of the gun. This time, on the top of his head. Blood squirt all over the place and ran down the front of his face.

"You better speak up Waters, before my man gets pissed," Ming said with a smile on his face. "I smoked it Ming, but I'll pay you back," Waters explained as the blood poured out his mouth and onto his white T-shirt.

"I know you will," Ming said as he looked down at him.

Ras grabbed Waters by his T-shirt, ripping it as he pulled him up, and twisted his arm behind his back. I could hear bones snapping as Waters let out a scream. His little girl continued to cry as her father got his ass waxed. Someone knocked on the door.

"You expectin' someone," Ras asked?

"It's probably my lady, Water said sobbingly. I sent her to the store."

Ras walked him to the door to make sure.

"Ask who it is," Ras whispered. "Who is it," Waters asked angrily? "It's Jeanna, open the fuckin' door."

Slowly, Waters opened the door. The light from the sun exposed his bloody T-shirt.

"What the fuck -"

Ras grabbed Jeanna by her hair and pulled her into the house. A girl accompanying Jeanna held onto her arm and was pulled in as well. Ras slammed the door behind them, and pushed Waters between the two of them as he pointed his gun at Waters' head.

Two For Five

Ras looked at both girls and asked, "y'all help him smoke our shit?"

Jeanna's girlfriend said with fear in her voice, "I just ran into her at the store, I don't know nothin' about what y'all talkin' about."

Ras motioned with his gun for them to move into the living room.

"Sit your asses down on the couch."

"Y'all tellin' us y'all ain't smoke our shit with him," Chase asked?

"Nuh," both girls said.

"Stop fuckin' lying. He ain't smoke this shit by himself, Ming spouted. Empty y'alls pockets." "I ain't got nothin' but some change from the store", Jenna remarked.

"How much is that," Ming asked?

"Just some change."

Ras started unzipping his pants, and told Jeanna to come here. She hesitated. He reached over the coffee table and literally pulled her ass across, knocking the table over as he did.

He threw her down on the ground, held the gun to her head and told her, "if y'all don't start tellin' us the fuckin' truth, my dick ain't the only thing you gonna be suckin' on."

Waters started copping a plea.

"My girl gets her check in the morning for a 'lil over seven hundred dollars. That's what I was gonna use to pay you with. Don't do that to my girl. I'll pay you your money Ming. Don't let him do that to my girl"

"I need my money now." Ming said. You thought I wasn't gonna find your ass, didn't you? To top it off, y'all smoked my shit. You think I'm gonna let that shit slide?

"I ain't have nothin' to do with this," Jenna's girlfriend said.

"Shut the fuck up," Ras screamed.

She starts crying.

"Bitch if you don't shut the fuck up and stop that fuckin' crying, you ain't gonna cry the rest of your natural life."

All you could hear was her snifflin, trying to hold back the tears.

"Y'all want these bitches to freak y'all off," Waters asked?

"I don't want no crack head bitch suckin' my dick, fuck on you mind, Ming replied. All I want is my money."

Ras pulled out his abnormally sized penis and shoved it in Jeanna's mouth.

Tears rolled down Jeanna's face as Ras forced her to do him.

"This bitch knows how to handle her business," Ras said, as his hips thrust back and forth, choking her with every stroke.

Ming looked down at Waters and said, "I got something' for you to smoke."

Ming pulled out a plastic bag that had what looked to be crack in it.

"Put this in your stem," Ming ordered.

Two For Five

Waters put a rock in his stem and lit it. It sizzled as he put the flame to it. He took a pull. The smoke quickly moved towards his slightly parted lips.

"This ain't crack," Waters remarked.

"Keep fuckin' smokin'," Ming demanded.

When he inhaled all the smoke, Ming told him to hold it until he told him to blow it out. Waters eyes rolled back in his head and he began to shake uncontrollably. Jeanna's girlfriend became hysterical as she watched Waters fall over on the floor.

"Please don't hurt me, she kept saying, I ain't have nothing to do with this shit.

"You do now, Ming commented. It's your turn to smoke."

Ming passed her one of the stems sitting on the table. Her hands shook as she reached for it. "Put it to your mouth," Ming demanded. She held the stem to her mouth but refused to smoke. Ming ordered her to take a pull but she continued to defy him. Finally, he grabbed her hand to put the stem in her mouth and flicked the lighter.

She still refused to take a pull. Ming, out of anger, slapped the stem into her mouth breaking it as it disappeared in a mixture of blood and spit.

Ming walked towards the door but turned around to kick Waters in the face. Then Ras, while trying to put his penis back in his pants, started stomping Waters and beating him with the butt of the gun until he lay motionless on the floor. Chase grabbed a bat that was in the corner of the living room, and hit Waters on the head twice, splitting it completely open. Chase ran upstairs to ransack the house. When he came back down, he was carrying a 19-inch color TV, and a brand new Nintendo computer game.

"That's my daughters stuff," Jeanna yelled.

"Now you know how it feels to have someone steal from you," Chase replied.

Before we left, Ming instructed Jeanna, "have this bitch ass nigga up and ready to work by 10 tonight.

Jeanna looked over at her man laying on the floor bleeding.

"You still gonna make him work?"

Yeah bitch. That nigga stole from me. You wanna take his place? Have his ass ready, like I said. You heard?"

Me, Chase, and Ras stood on the front steps waiting for Ming to come out. When he did, he asked," y'all hungry? Lets go to the Rib Shack and get somethin' to eat."

Ras laughed, and said, "I'm headin' to my yard, check y'all later, aight."

That incident is what lead me to believe, once you in this game, ain't no leaving without war wounds. Waters was proof positive of that. That shit had me hyped.

I saw the power that little whie rock carried and I wanted to find out more. When Ming and me got in the car I asked him, "is this the shit you and Chase been dealin' with since I've been gone?"

"Yeah, but now that you're home, I'll have more time to step to them brothers' that been doin' dumb shit like tappin' our packs, or ma'fuckas' thinkin' I ain't got time to run they ass down if they run off with our shit. I told you Niko, shits 'bout to change real quick when it comes to keepin' shit tight out here. You see my man Ras ain't no joke and will *murder* a ma'fucka if he had to. Niko , I feel it in my bones, we 'bout to take this game to another level. All I need you to do is handle your business and make sure brothers be where they suppose to be. Oh, I almost forgot, I got you a ride. They suppose to deliver it to your house sometime tomorrow."

Chapter Four

I'm moving around on my own now. Ming leased a Black Jeep Grand Cherokee for me, under the companies' name. I've gotten familiar with all the locations I need to pick up cash from and all our workers have gotten to know me as well. The barbershop on Foch Boulevard became my base of operation. From there, I kept track of all the money that came in. It also became a dispatch point for brothers that wanted to sling for us. Brothers hustling on the block would tell prospective employees to come see me if they wanted to be put on the payroll. My beeper would go off damn near every two minutes or so. Sometimes it wasn't just to pick up money. I started hearing complaints from our street crews telling me Ming had them waiting for hours for the next pack. I noticed a difference in him as well. He didn't return my calls as quick as he used to, and when he did, he sounded like he was drowsy or just waking up. That shit had me wondering, what the fuck's going on with my partner? I called Chase to see if he had heard from him, or noticed any changes in his behavior as well. Chase said he stopped calling him after he saw he wasn't returning his calls. I connected with Chase to figure out how we could keep our workers constantly supplied. Especially since it's just him and me doing all the running round, and at the same time, I'm worrying about what's up with Ming. I never wanted to get this close to the hustle end of the business but Ming's my man, and until I find out what's happening with him, I gotta step up my game and keep shit moving. I go by his house on a regular, ring the bell, but nobody answers. A week ago, around three in the morning, I was in bed with my girl when the telephone rang. It was Ming sounding real fucked up. I could hardly understand his words.

What I did hear was him asking me to come to his house as soon as I could. I asked him was everything okay but before I got an answer, he hung up the phone. I got up, sure not to wake my lady, but she got up anyway. She asked me, "where you goin' this time of night' Daddy?"

"Ming just called and asked me to come by his house. He didn't sound too good."

I didn't want to say nothing to you 'til I was sure myself, but my girl told me she saw Ming the other night on Merrick stumbling to his car. When she approached him, he didn't even recognize her. She said he was fumbling around with his car keys and nodding off before he finally got the door open. Then she said after he got in, he sat there sniffing what might've been coke, but because of the way he was nodding, she thought it might be dope. I told her I'd find out what the deal was when I saw him." I gave her a kiss and told her to go back to bed. She called me as I walked toward the door, "baby, you be careful out there and call me to let me know what's going on, alright?"

"Yeah, babe, go back to sleep, I won't be long."

As I drove over to his house, which was in an exclusive section of Queens called Laurelton Estates, all kinds of thoughts came to mind. I recalled what my girl told me about her girlfriend seeing Ming nodding and fumbling around with his keys. That shit had me fucked up. My beeper went off but no phone number came up. The numbers that appeared looked like an address. It wasn't familiar to me. My beeper went off again. This time a number came up and at the end of it was 911. I pulled over to the nearest phone, got out, and looked at the number on my pager. I didn't recognize the number either.

I figured it was one of my workers beeping me for another pack. But, that couldn't be, I left everybody with enough drugs to hold them for the night. I called the number. A lady answered.

"Hello," she said.

I didn't recognize the voice.

"Who's this?" I asked.

"Is this Niko?"

"Yeah, who's this?"

"I'm a friend of Ming's," she said. "I think you should come by my house as quick as possible to see about your man."

Again I asked, "who's this?"

"My name is Precious. I live on 89th Avenue and 153rd . It's the building on the corner. You know where I'm talking about?"

"Yeah, that's where all the dope heads be, right?"

"Yeah," she replied.

"What the fuck he doin' over there?" I asked.

"You don't know?"

"Know what?" I asked angrily.

"Your partner's fucked up off that diesel."

"What diesel? What the fuck you talking about?

My tone got angrier and angrier as we spoke.

"Bitch listen, I don't know what the fuck you talkin' about but I'm almost there."

"What street you on?" She asked"

"I'm about three blocks away."

"I'm on my way downstairs," she said. "I'll be standing in front the building when you get here, okay?"

"Yeah, make sure your ass is out there when I get there, understand?"

I hung up the phone and called Chase. The phone rang about ten times before he picked up. "Chase."

"Yeah, who's this?"

"Niko, wake the fuck up and meet me on 89th Avenue and 153rd Street right now."

"Why, what's up?" He asked.

I could hear the sleepiness in his voice.

"Don't ask questions, just get the fuck up and get here. I expect to see you in fifteen minutes, understand?"

"Yeah, yeah, I heard you; I'm coming."

"You still on the fuckin' phone, hang the motherfucker up and get your ass down here."

"Aight, aight Niko, calm down. I'm comin', I'm comin'."

I slammed the phone down, got back in my jeep, and drove to the front of the building. I waited there but didn't see the girl in front of the building like I asked her to be. I looked at my beeper to see if I missed any calls but the only numbers I saw were the ones I already answered. I looked up at the address on the building and the numbers on my beeper, the numbers matched. I got back in my Jeep and pulled around the corner to park. I walked back to the front of the building and looked around just to make sure I wasn't being set-up or something. Just then Chase pulled up. As he got out his car he had both his guns drawn ready to blast anything that moved.

"What up Niko?" Everything aight?"

"I don't know yet, I just got here."

He asked again, "what up, why you rush me down here? I thought you had beef or somethin' nigga." "Nah, I'm cool, but our boy may not be."

"Who, Ming?"

"Yeah. Who the fuck else?"

"Tell me what's up," Chase asked?

"I'm waiting for this chick to come downstairs that lives in this building. She called me and said I should come over here to check on Ming."

Chase and I stood in front the building looking in every direction not knowing what to expect or what to look for. All I knew was Ming called me earlier and asked me to come to his house to check on him. Then this chick called me telling me Ming's over her house. Either way we're here to check on our man. I didn't mention the stuff my girl told me. As Chase and I continued to look around, he recognized the area we were in and yelled out Ming's name.

"What the fuck he doin' over here," Chase asked? "I don't know kid but, we about to find out." Neither he nor I wanted to believe or think the thoughts we were having, but we had to ask ourselves some questions. What was he doing on this side of town? I heard this old saying somewhere that went like this, "if it walks like a duck, quacks like a duck, smells like a duck, then damn it, it's a duck". That helped me to put things in perspective and understand why we were where we were. Just the thought of him being strung out, brought tears to my eyes. Ming's my man from way back. We grew up together.

What the fuck was he doing over here in the first fucking place? Chase looked at me like he was about to loose it. I had to stay focused, and keep us both on point just in case this was a set-up. The door to the building opened and a middle-aged woman walked towards us. She called out my name.

"Niko?" Which one of you is Niko?"

"Who you?" Chase asked.

"I'm the girl that called you."

I stepped closer to her and said, "I'm Niko."

She stepped back.

"Where's Ming," I asked?

"He's upstairs in my apartment."

"What floor you live on?"

"The third floor," she quickly answered, "apartment 3E, right here in the front of the building." She pointed to a third floor window that was half-open with the curtains blowing in and out from the wind.

"What's going on up there," Chase asked?

She told us Ming had been by her house all day getting high. While she was speaking, gunshots rang out. We ducked for cover. Then we saw Ming's body come crashing to the ground. Chase and I pointed our guns to the windows above us. Chase reached out to pull Ming closer but he was too far to reach. I grabbed Chase by the back of his shirt and pulled him back towards me. At the same time, I pulled the girl by her arm and pointed my gun to her head.

"Who the fucks in your apartment," I asked?

She started stumbling with her words. I asked her again, but this time I cocked the hammer back on my nickel-plated .380. I heard Chase pull the hammer back on his as well.

I looked dead in her eyes and told her, "if you don't tell me what the fuck's going on up there, you gonna be lying right next to my man. So start talking."

She started crying. Chase slapped her and told her to snap out that shit and talk.

"How long he been over here," Chase asked?

In between sniffles, she said Ming had been coming over to her house for the past two months and that some of the dope fiends in the neighborhood knew he spent a lot of money and thought they could roll him for his drugs and cash.

"Stop!" Chase said, "I don't wanna hear no more. You set my man up, didn't you?"

She quickly put her hand in the air, and said, "my hand to God, I wouldn't do that to Ming." I jumped in and asked, "then who them motherfuckers' in your apartment?"

"Me and Ming went to the Liquor Store to get something to drink, and when we got off the elevator, these guys jumped out with their guns drawn and forced us into my apartment."

"That's bullshit," Chase said. "How the fuck they knew he was over here unless you told 'em." You could see the terror in her eyes. Ming's body began twitching. A woman looking out her apartment window on the first floor asked, "is that boy alright?" She offered to call the police for me.

I asked her if I could call them myself. She passed the phone through the window but I didn't call the police.

called Big Ras who lived five minutes away. The phone rang

for a while before he picked up.

"Who dat?" Ras asked.

His voice sounded like he was in a deep sleep.

"It's me, Niko,"

"What go on my bredren?"

"I need you to come to 89th Avenue and 153rd Street right now. Somebody just shot Ming."

You could hear in his voice the news had woke his ass right the fuck up.

"Say no more knotty," Ras said, "me soon come, ya hear?" "Me soon come."

By the time I hung up the phone, I heard police sirens.

Chase pulled me by my arm and said, "we need to get the hell outta here, Niko."

I still had a firm grip on the girl's arm and pulled her along as Chase and I made our way to the Jeep parked around the corner. I swung open the back door and threw her ass in headfirst.

"Where's the keys?" Chase asked.

"I got 'em in my pocket."

I reached in my pocket, took the keys out and flung them over the roof of the Jeep. Chase hurried to open the door because the sirens were getting closer. "I didn't have anything to do with your partner getting shot," the girl kept saying.

"Shut the fuck up." Chase yelled. "You gonna hang out with us 'til we find out who them niggas' were in your apartment, and when we do, we better not find out you had anything to do with this shit."

Three motorcycles pulled up to the light. It was Ras and a couple of his boys. Chase rolled the window down and said, "swing around the block and meet us on Hillside."

The first police car pulled up just as we were pulling off. When we got to Hillside, Ras got off his bike and walked to the driver's side of the Jeep.

Chase rolled his window down and said, "we gotta get the hell outta here, but I need you and your crew to hang out and see if the cops come out the building with anybody."

Ras said, "don't worry, I'll be right here 'til they leave." He looked in the back of the Jeep and said, "who's that?"

"That's the bitch that set up Ming," Chase replied.

Ras opened the back door and pulled out his gun. He grabbed the girl by her hair and stuck the gun in her face and asked her, "you know them niggas' that shot my man?"

"I told y'all, I don't know them guys but I can point them out."

I turned around in my seat and asked her, "where they be at?"

"They usually be hanging out by the stores over on 153rd Street", she said.

"Wait for the cops to leave before you break out," I explained to Ras, and "make sure you peep if they come out the building with anybody."

"No problem boss," Ras replied.

Before we pulled off, Chase gave Ras the keys to his car and told him to park it by his house and he'll pick it up later. Chase and I headed back to Laurelton.

On the way, Chase stopped the Jeep, put it in park, walked around to the back door on the passengers' side and opened it. The look in his eyes was something I never seen before.

He grabbed the girl by the shirt, pulled her towards him and punched her in the face. She slumped unconscious on the back seat. Chase walked back around to the drivers' side, got back in, and pulled off.

"Why you do that?" I asked.

"Cause I don't want that bitch to see where we takin' her," he replied.

We pulled up in front of his house on 138th Avenue and 224th Street. He backed the Jeep into the driveway, got out and opened the garage door. He searched through his pockets to find the keys to the trunk of the car that sat in the garage. After he opened the trunk he came back to the Jeep and pulled the girl out by her feet. Her head bounced on the ground as he dragged her over to the car. I got out to help him lift her up. Once we had her in the trunk, Chase slammed the trunk shut and closed the garage door.

"What if somebody hears her yelling?" I asked.

"I know what to do," Chase said.

He walked to the side of the garage and opened the gate that lead to the backyard. I heard a door open in the back of the house. Then I heard dogs barking. I looked around the side of the garage, and Chase was coming back to the front with two big ass pit bulls.

"What they for?" I asked. "To keep nosey asses away from the house and to kill any noise she might make." We got back in the Jeep and drove back to 89th Avenue to find out if Ras had found out anything new.

When we pulled up to the building, cops were everywhere. We parked in the middle of the block on 153rd Street and walked to where Ras and his crew were standing.

"What's up Ras?" Chase asked.

"Everything cool boss."

"Did the cops bring anybody out yet?" I asked.

"Nuh my bredren," Ras replied.

I looked across the street and saw Ming's body still lying on the ground covered by a bloodstained white sheet.

"Why they haven't picked him up yet?" Chase asked angrily.

I turned to him and said, "I don't know kid. Listen, we ain't gonna hang out here too much longer.

Chase told Ras and his crew to breakout and we'd call them if we needed them.

"Let's go across the street to look at Ming for the last time," Chase suggested.

"We can't, I said, we about to leave and find out from that chick who them niggas' were that shot him." As we drove back to the house, there weren't many words said between us. The silence told it all. Both of us were hurt by the fact that, first, our partner was dead, and secondly, we found out something about him we would've never thought. Those thoughts had us both fucked up. When we got back to the house, the sun was just coming up. Chase and I decided we would wait until it got dark to drive this chick around to see what happens. We left her ass in the trunk of the car in the garage until we got up. Later that night we went back to the garage to get her up so we could drive around to see if she could point out the punk ass motherfuckers' that shot Ming. The first two days we felt she was bullshittin' us. Chase and I were getting pissed. On the third night, around ten O'clock, we were driving down South Road over by Forty Projects with this chick in the back seat. As we turned onto Sutphin

Boulevard, she asked us to slow down.

"Why?" Chase asked.

"I think I see one of the guys that shot your partner," she responded.

"Where, where," I asked.

"Right there," she said, pointing her finger at a group of guys hanging out on the corner of Liberty

Avenue and Sutphin. The windows of our Jeep were tinted making it easy for us to rollup on them without being noticed. We parked a few feet away from them.

"That's them right there, both of them," she said.

One of them was nodding so bad I thought he was gonna fall over.

The other guy was talking to four other brothers' around him.

"I'm gonna call Ras, Chase said, and have him meet us over here."

He got out the Jeep and walked over to a payphone. As he walked past, nobody even looked his way. Chase stayed on the phone for about five minutes before he returned to the Jeep. As he got back in, he said Ras and his crew would be there in a couple of minutes.

"What y'all gonna do with me?" the girl asked.

Chase and I looked at each other.

"We haven't decided yet."

"I showed y'all the guys you were looking for, so why don't you let me go?"

"We still don't know if you had anything to do with this shit," Chase responded. Until we're sure, you stayin' with us. So sit the fuck back and shut the fuck up."

The sounds of motorcycles were getting closer. As they pulled up, Chase and I got out the Jeep. Ras parked his bike behind us. The other two brothers from his crew parked on the corner. Ras walked up with a spliff hanging out his mouth and slapped us both five.

"What go on my bredred," Ras greeted.

"Ain't nothin' knottie."

Ras looked over at the guys standing in front of the store and asked," them the bad asses that shot Ming?"

"Yeah, the girl pointed them out," I replied. "We got this, my youth, Ras assured. Don't worry. We got this, you 'ere?"

Ras motioned for one of his crew to stand directly in front the five guys by the store.

"Leave my youth! Cause we bout to lick off some bum ba' clot shots round this pussyclot," Ras said with his deep Jamaican accent.

Chase and I pulled off. Before we got to the corner, I heard gunshots. The shots were so loud I had to look around to see how far we were from them. We drove back to Chases' house where we dragged the girl out the Jeep and once again, threw her back in the trunk. Chase and I stood outside deciding what to do with her.

"We can't keep her alive, Chase said."

"I know. Leave her ass in the trunk and drive the car to a deserted area," I suggested.

"What if somebody finds her," Chase asked?

"So what you wanna do, off her?"

"I'll handle this. You go on home," Chase said.

"You sure?"

"Yeah, I'll take care of this."

I got in my Jeep and drove off. That's the last I ever heard about her.

Chapter Five

The day Ming's body was to be viewed, I got to the funeral parlor before the body was placed in the viewing room. The viewing took place at a Funeral Parlor on Linden Boulevard. When I got there the Funeral Director, Mr. Alvin Best, greeted me at the entrance. As he shook my hand, I couldn't help but noticed how cold his hands were. I pried my hand from his and asked him had anyone else showed up.

"No," he said in a deep voice that sounded as spooky as his handshake felt. He asked me if I wanted to see the deceased. I nodded my head in agreement. He led the way to a room called *"the viewing area"*.

Do you mind if I have a few moments alone, I asked?

He said, "of course not, take all the time you need." I walked up to the open casket. Ming looked like he was sleeping with his arms by his side. He had on a blue pinstriped suit Chase and I brought him. I stood there, looking down at him. In my mind, I was expecting him to get up, but I knew that wouldn't happen. I touched his hand. He felt cold and stiff as a board. Tears started rolling down my face. At first, I tried to fight it. I needed to keep my head together. But I couldn't fight it any longer. Then it all hit me. Tears streamed down my face and I couldn't stop crying, I just couldn't stop. It was just he and I. Together, like we were most of our life. My thoughts drifted back to when we grew up. We did everything together. Chased the girls when we were in elementary school. Caught them in junior high school. Ran trains on them when we reached high school. Tears kept running down my face. I kept repeating over, and over in my head, he's dead, he's dead.

My fucking man is dead! I thought about when I first came home from upstate. I remembered it like it was yesterday.

I was about to close the door to my house when a car pulled up. The windows were tinted so I couldn't see the occupants. Both the driver and the passengers' door opened at the same time. The back of the drivers' head slightly passed the roof of the car and the right foot of the passenger reached for the pavement. I still hadn't figured out who this was. I hadn't seen my boys in a long time. With his back facing me, the driver yelled out, "is that my nigga?" The passenger stood up and said, "welcome home kid." Their voices still fresh in my mind. We grew up together from the time we were in pampers. My sister baby-sat us when our parents went to work. Ming and I were the closest. We lived two houses down from each other. We did everything together, everything. We played ball together, got in trouble together. Drank our first beers together. You name it. We did it, together. We met Chase when we were in elementary school. He was playing basketball by himself in the school yard. Ming decided to take his ball. He wasn't having it. He put up a good fight that day. Ming and I weren't bullies or nothing, we just wanted to fuck with him and see what he'd do. After that, Chase was always down with whatever Ming and I got into. I remember the handshakes we exchanged. How we slapped each other five and reminisced about days long past. They were glad to see me and I was glad to see them. Their showing up as they did, showed me how much they missed me and I was glad to be back with my boys. I remember questioning Ming about where he got the money to buy the car he was driving. "We been getting' paid nigga," he boasted.

And when the time's right, we need you to get this money with us. But right now, we just glad to see your black ass home."

He gave me a welcome home gift from the both of them. He reached in his pocket, pulled out a hand full of money, and gave me twenty-five hundred dollars. "That's so you don't have to ask nobody for shit, Ming said. We got you."

Chase, repeated, "yeah we got you, kid."

"What your mama cooking for dinner, Ming asked? I know your family hooked up a big meal for your ass. What's up with the grub?"

My moms came to the door to see where I was. When she saw who I was talking to, you could see how happy she was to see us together again. Mama called us into the house. As we walked past, both Ming and Chase leaned over to give my moms a kiss on the cheek and asked how she was feeling. My moms responded by giving them both a hug and a kiss and saying in a motherly tone, "I'm alright, baby. I told you guys he'd be home soon." Then she turned to me and said, "they've been ringing the bell and knocking on the door since ten this morning, wanting to know if you got home yet. Then mama said, I'm so glad to see you all together again. Y'all come on in and sit down and have something to eat. Deborah should be finished cooking by now."

The Funeral Director opened the door of the viewing room to tell me that someone else was here to see the deceased. I wiped the tears from my eyes and pulled myself together so I could greet whoever came to see my man for the last time. It was Chase and Big Ras.

Ras asked me, "you alright, star?"

"No doubt, knottie, I'm good, I'm good."

I could tell Chase wasn't going to make it two seconds without breaking down. I reached out my arms and he grabbed me with all his might and said, "Niko, I miss him yo. I'm fucked up right now."

Two For Five

I patted him on his back and told him, "keep your head up kid, we gonna get through this." He broke down, just like I said he would and so did Ras.

Chapter Six

Two days after we buried Ming, I was sitting in my office looking at some pictures me, Ming and Chase had taken since I'd come home. All I kept thinking is his ass would still be here if he hadn't been over at that chick's house sniffing that shit. On the one hand, I was angry he allowed himself to get caught up like that. On the other hand, I felt like abusing *anybody* who used drugs. It didn't matter what they used. Crack, dope, smoke. Well, maybe not the potheads. But anyone else, fuck 'em. Our motto became, "You smoke, you buy, you live, you die". 'And it better be from us! The crews we had hustling on the streets were grinding harder than ever. Chase and I put together twelve teams in different locations, pumping day and night all over Queens. If you didn't see us, beep us, and we'll deliver whatever you need. We didn't focus on just one group of people that got high. We went after them all. If you smoked crack, we got you. If you smoked weed, we got that too. If you skin-popped or sniffed dope, bring it. I didn't have any remorse for a motherfucker that got high. I ain't feel shit for nobody for that matter. Hookers out there slinging their stink ass for a hit, hurry up and finish, so you can bring that money. Brothers out there catching "vicks", run that cash, we want it all. No change and no shorts from nobody. I didn't care if a motherfucker had four dollars and ninety-nine cents. Get the rest, and come back correct. If a crack head had to steal his mama's TV set, so what, I didn't care how they got their money, just as long as you spent it with us. There was this hooker name Rochelle, who was a dollar fifty short for a two for five deal. She was thirsty as a fuck for a hit. She slobbed the knob of every last brother in my crew for two rocks. If she didn't care, why should I? That's how I felt.

Fuck 'em. Some of my boys would beat the shit out of custies if they brought from someplace else. All this shit's affecting my relationship with my girl. I'm spending more time in the streets than with her. We argue over the stupidest of things and they always end with me walking out the door. I remember the question Ming asked me one day. Do I ever feel like just saying fuck it sometimes? Hell yeah. Right about now, more than ever. It didn't really matter about the money. Even though the money was rolling, there was something missing, and I couldn't put my finger on it. I would hang out with the fellas for days at a time, not calling home to let my girl know I'm alright. Ming's death really fucked my head up and I couldn't shake the feeling. This old-timer named Mister Bimms, who hung out on the block

by the liquor store on 221st Street and Merrick, told me he'd been watching me and thought he should give me some words of advise.

"Boy, I notice that you ain't been the same since that other nappy headed nigga got kilt. But let me tell you somethin', you still here 'lil nigga. So snap out that shit. Walkin' round here acting' like you ready to fight the world. I see ya boy. Don't think I don't. No sir. You's a damn fool if you think that sellin' that shit gonna make life better for you. You need to take your ass on home to your family before you end up like

your partner. You hear me boy?"

"Yes sir, I hear you."

Mister Bimms continued to kick it to me.

"I know you hurtin' right now boy. I remember you and that 'lil nigga Ming before you niggas even knew your own name. I watched y'all grow up round here and I know what y'all was out here doing.

But you got to let that shit go and move on with yourself. Now gimme three dollars so I can buy me somethin' to drink. I know you got it."

"Yeah, I got it Mister B." I reached in my pocket and gave him a ten-dollar bill and told him, "thanks, I needed to hear that."

"Anytime boy. You come see Mister B anytime you need."

Two For Five

"Alright Mister B, take care."

Aside from the stench of Vodka that filled my nose, the thoughts he left me with had me thinking. The shit you do to others, will surely come back to bite you on the ass.

Chapter Seven

For the past few weeks, I haven't been home, at least not consistently. My girl has been blowing up my pager trying to reach me. At the end of each page, she leaves 911. I know she's worrying about me but I just can't get it together. Right about now, I'm really not trying to hear her. I'm having a hard enough time just dealing with what's going on in my head. Ming's death has me twisted. I miss my brother. Chase and I have been running around like chickens with our heads cut off keeping tabs on our workers and making sure they out there moving our shit like they suppose to. At this point, everything's going smooth. All our workers' are doing their thing. On Merrick and 228th street, the crew we got over there has been moving product like crazy. For the past couple of months, they've been turning in, on a consistent basis, about five thousand dollars a night. On 140th and Foch, in front of the grocery store, the crew over there has been handling their business as well. Every night, when I go to pick up cash from them, it's always four thousand dollars or better. One of the reasons we've been having this kind of rhythm is because we keep our crews well supplied. I learned a long time ago, to keep custies loyal you got to always be available, never run out of product, and always have the biggest and the best product out. I would have a smoker test our product to make sure we got it good. If I didn't see them tweekin', I knew I needed to change the package. Out of each crew, one person reported directly to me. It's their responsibility to make sure their count was correct. This way they don't run out of product. If they needed more work, they called me, and I'd make sure Chase brought them whatever they needed.

This way I could handle other things. I tell my crews to remember some simple rules. First, maintain control at all times, and make sure your lookouts are on their damn job. Second, don't try to serve too many people at the same time. This way nobody can pass you any funny money. Too many times, I've seen where fiends clipped of the ends of dollar bills and taped them up with ten dollar notes. Third, when you get down to your last twenty pieces call me and I'll make sure you get whatever you need. Lastly, motherfuckers that bring you money today can be the same motherfuckers that turn your ass in tomorrow. So treat people with some respect regardless of the fact they get high. It's because of them we got shit flowing the way we do. My mind is stressed out from having to keep track of all this. Making sure my workers are on point and doing their thing and keeping them supplied with product. Picking up and counting money every night and making sure ain't no shorts. Then getting up early in the morning to open up the shops and make sure things over there are running smoothly. At times, it's a bit much. But deep down, I love this shit. My Parole Officer has been on my ass cause she's noticing every week when I turn in my pay stub it's more than what she makes. I think she's pissed off about that. Maybe even a little jealous. She made mention of that the other day when I went to see her.

"How is it you can afford these expensive clothes, and drive around in a car nicer than mine? You say you manage a barbershop?

"Yeah, I told her. The owner makes damn sure he takes good care of me". If she only knew, I'm the damn owner.

"Nevertheless, I work hard for mine. That's why I can afford the things you see me with, I explained. And besides, I know the value of a dollar and how important it is to put a few away for a rainy day."

Within the past month, Chase opened a couple of new drug spots in Lefrak City. I opened a barbershop under the name "Nappy Naps" in the same area. We hooked that spot up sweet. Beautiful hardwood floors with freshly polished oak wood paneling and on every wall pictures of famous Black leaders. We found a huge space in the basement of one of the buildings, and were able to put in ten barber's chairs. In the back of the shop, we set up a beauty salon complete with hair washing sinks and hairdryers. Built into the wall was a wide screen T.V. connected to the stereo system giving the shop that surround sound you hear in theaters. If I say so myself, we hooked that spot up to the max. Every Saturday, between the hours of nine in the morning 'til three in the afternoon, we charged five dollars per cut for kids under fifteen. This way, I figured, we could build up our clientele. You know how it is in the projects. Everybody's looking for some kind of deal. Single moms with a house full of nappy headed boys needs to know who the best barber is, and at the same time, find the best price. Young cats trying to stay dipped for the girls' would jump on the opportunity to keep their wig tight.

We provided that. I found out about Lefrak City through my mans' and them who use to sling over there before they got knocked. They told me I should run through and check out the cash flow. So I did. One Saturday afternoon, Chase and I strolled through the

main strip of Lefrak city, which is 57th Avenue. Nice day out. People were moving around doing the things most people do on any given Saturday.

Going shopping, doing laundry, or just stretching their legs, and socializing with other members in the community.

We got off the expressway, turned onto Junction Boulevard, and stopped at a red light at the corner of Junction and Horace Harding Expressway. While we waited for the light to turn green, we were amazed at how big the complex is, and wondered how many people must be getting high in there. The light turned green and we continued up Junction Boulevard until we found a

parking space on the corner of Junction and 57th Avenue. We parked the car, got out and walked through to 99th street, which runs parallel to Junction Boulevard. 57th Avenue is the connecting street between the two. It covers about seven or eight long blocks, which is the entire length of Lefrak City's huge complex. As we walked through, we took notice of who was posted up where, and who looked like they were out there hustling and getting paper. From what I could tell, most of the brothers hung out in front of the stores directly across the street from the buildings. Up the street, the Jamaicans posted up selling their weed. They hung out in packs and tried to conceal their dealings. To me they were too noticeable. They also dealt with too many white boys. Sometimes it was hard to distinguish the cops from the customers. As we continued our tour, a lot of pretty women passed us. Chase stopped a few, trying to get their numbers.

But, there was this one chick we passed, who looked like she got high. I can always spot somebody who's getting high by the way they carry themselves. Usually, a person getting high walks with their head down as though they're searching the ground for an easy come off by finding that lost bag somebody dropped.

When we approached her, she looked up and asked, "hey, don't I know y'all?"

"Nuh, we ain't from around here."

"Y'all from Brooklyn?"

"Nuh, we from out here in Queens."

She continued to question us. "Could either of y'all spare a dollar, or some change, so I can get somethin' to eat?"

I don't have any change, I replied.

It amazes me how people always try to run game and think you ain't up on shit. Chase didn't even bother to look.

Instead, he asked, "you get high?"

"Why", she questioned while putting her hands on her hips.

"I just asked baby, nothing personal."

She came back with some slick shit. "Is grits groceries? Is eggs poultry?

Hell yeah I get high. Why, you got somethin'?"

I could tell right off, she's one of them slick ass chicks. Chase just shook his head and pulled out a plastic bag he had stashed in his pants to give her a sample of our product. I could see the thirst in her eyes as he reached in the bag to find a nice size rock. As soon as she saw the size of the rock he was gonna give her, her eyes damn near popped out her head.

"Damn those shits look big, she commented. What y'all selling them for?"

"What they look like, Chase asked?"

"Twenties," she asked curiously?

"Nuh, these nickels'."

"Stop lying!   Them shits ain't nickels," she said defiantly.

"Why you say that," Chase asked as the rock rolled around in his hand.

What's the size of the rocks they got around here? They smaller?"

"Hell yeah, they small. Them shits ain't no nickels, that's for sure. Y'all know what I could sell this shit for right now?"

Her eyes focused intently on the rock she held in her hand. As I looked over at Chase, I could see dollars signs forming in his eyes.

"Nuh, What," Chase asked?

"I could break this down, she explained, and sell it as dimes and make damn near thirty dollars off this shit.

"Y'all aint' from around her, are y'all?"

"You asked us that already and I told you, no! We from Saint Albans."

"Word? My moms lives in Cambria Heights by the expressway. Y'all need to come over here with this shit, exposing the rock she held in the palm of her hand. "Y'all kill these lame ass niggas' around here, selling that tiny ass garbage they got."

I pulled her closer, and asked, you know everybody around here that smokes?

"Yeah," she answered.

"Do they have their own places or is there somewhere everybody goes to get high?"

"Most people I know got jobs and usually stay in their own apartments to smoke. Then you have them thirsty ass ma'fuckers' that smoke anywhere they can. Smoking on staircases, behind parked cars, anywhere, you feel me? That shit give smokers' like me a bad name."

She continued to explain the difference between her and other smokers.

"Some people, like me, smoke, others smoke so hard, they don't smoke, they *moke!* On the real, I can take you, right now, to a few spots where niggas be spendin' money."

Where they at, I asked?

"Right across the street, in that building, that building, that building. You look in any direction, you can find somebody that smokes crack."

Who lives in those spots, I asked?

"What you mean," She questioned?

I mean, are they older, younger, what?

The more questions I asked, the more she readily gave answers.

"They older, but they cool."

What kinda money they spend, I asked?

"This one trick I know, works for the Post Office, he likes to mess with the hoes out here. He got a good job, and a nice apartment, but smokes real fast. He'll spend anywhere between fifty to three hundred dollars on any given weekend, easily. During the week, she continued, he might get a couple of twenties after work but the weekends, it's on and poppin'. That's when I usually catch his ass. I make sure when I go to his house, around six in the evening, I bring his first hit so he can get open. Once I see his ass "tweekin", I know I got him. Sometimes, Kathy continued, I don't even have to do nothin' cause his dick won't get hard, but he keeps on smokin' and watching them short eyes flicks."

Short eyes, I asked, what the fuck is that?

She schooled me real quick. "Short eyes is x-rated movies. You know how y'all niggas' get when y'all get high. Y'all never heard of that shit before, she asked?

Nuh, I replied. Does he allow you to bring people to his house?

"As long as you got drugs, Kathy explained, that nigga's door is open like seven eleven." "He home now?" Chase asked. "Yeah," she replied.

You know if anybody else is up there? I asked.

"I don't know, I'm here with y'all. But we can check." "He drink beer or somethin'?" Chase questioned.

"Yeah, sometimes but most of the time he just wants to smoke crack. Why, you gonna buy some?"

"Maybe," Chase replied.

In order for you to introduce us, what we gotta give you? I asked.

"Cause y'all niggas' been straight with me, I'll tell you what. Y'all look out for me and I'll look out for you. I'll make sure that every motherfucker that smokes crack knows y'all got it good. Every five nickels I sell for y'all, y'all give me one for myself. Deal?"

"Deal, Chase agreed, and gave her a pound.

As we walked towards the buildings, she asked us our names. At first, Chase hesitated. Then he said, "that's not important right now."

Thinking quickly on her feet, Kathy asked, "then who I'm gonna say y'all are when he comes to the door."

My names Niko. This my partner, Chase.

She shook both our hands and began repeating it over and over as though she was trying to embed our names in her brain. As we crossed the street, somebody called out her name. She stopped to see who it was. Chase and I kept walking.

"Hold up a minute, she yelled, I know him. He probably got a few dollars and wants me to cop for him. Y'all wanna deal with him?"

Chase stopped for a second and asked her to find out what he wanted. I looked over my shoulder to see if the person she was talking to looked like a cop or a smoker.

The guy called her name again and caught up to her and they began talking. Chase and I were too far away to hear what they were saying, but I could almost imagine what the conversation was about. I saw some hand-to-hand maneuvers and it looked like he passed her some money. He looked to be in his early thirties, dark skinned, wearing a pair of dirty jeans with a light blue shirt that was stained with oil. I figured he must be a mechanic or something. Chase and I stopped to see what the deal was and to see if she was gonna bring us that money. We waited for her to finish her conversation. She walked away from the guy and made her way towards us. In her hand, I saw cash. As she walked up with a big smile on her face, she clutched a twenty-dollar bill tightly in her grip.

"See, I told y'all niggas'. Money just comes to a bitch like me. Gimme back ten dollars change" I looked at her and asked, "you don't want four of these, pointing to the rocks Chase held in his hand. She looked down at the rocks Chase was gonna sell her and thought for a second.

"Yeah alright. I sold that guy the rock y'all gave me and was tryin' to hold on to some money for myself. I need money too, but now that you mention it, can y'all give me five of those for twenty?

Chase and I looked at each other and probably thought the same shit. This bitch got game. Instead of me having one rock, she said, now I'll have five and can make a few dollars and still get high. I'm glad I ran into y'all," she concluded. Chase put five rocks in her hand and quickly snatched the money. She looked down at the rocks she had and said with a devilish gleam in her eyes, "let's go upstairs and see if this trick is home."

The three of us continued to walk towards the building.

When we got to the lobby of the building, she rang 11J. A voice over the intercom asked, "who is it?" The voice sounded deep.

"It's me, Kathy, buzz me in."

She pushed the door as the buzzer rang and we stepped through. As we approached the elevator, a tall dude and a lady were getting off the elevator and walking towards us.

"How y'all doing," Kathy greeted. Where y'all goin'?"

"To the store," the lady responded.

"Listen, if y'all need somethin', Kathy explained, I got it."

"What you got, the tall brother asked, the same garbage they sellin' across the street?"

"Nah man, I got some brand new shit."

"Let me see what you got," the lady asked skeptically.

Kathy showed her two of the rocks Chase had gave her and immediately the lady reached in her pocket and pulled out some money to make a purchase.

"How much you sellin' them for," the lady asked?

"Forty dollars for both," Kathy replied.

She pulled out two ten dollar bills and a five and turned to her man and asked, "do you have any money on you?

"Yeah, how much you need?"

"Gimme fifteen dollars," the lady said quickly.

"Here Kathy. count it. It's all there."

"I trust y'all, Kathy said. If y'all need some more, ring 11J that's where I'll be."

"Alright Kat, I'll holla at ya later."

Chase was holding the elevator for Kathy and me to step in. The doors opened to a long hallway. The lighting was bright allowing me to see clearly in both directions. From the distance, I could see someone standing in the doorway of an apartment. He looked to be about forty, slight build, wearing a bathrobe with burgundy pajamas and a pair of gold rimmed glasses that reflected the ceiling light off the lenses.

As we got to the apartment, Kathy said in a loud voice, "hi Jimmy, how you doin'?"

"I'm alright, he replied. What you come by for? I ain't got nothin'."

"Shut the fuck up Jimmy and let me in, Kathy demanded. I got somethin' for us to smoke and I want you to meet some friends of mine"

"Who they? Your cousins?"

"Nah, this is Chase and he's Niko. They got some fat ass twenties they sellin' and gave me one to smoke with you."

"You got somethin' to smoke," Jimmy asked curiously?

His eyes got wide as silver dollars when she showed him the rocks she had.

"Sit your ass down old man and let's take a hit," Kathy demanded.

"I got your old man," Jimmy replied while holding his crouch.

Chase and I noticed the drool oozing down Jimmy's chin as he waited for Kathy to pass him something to smoke. Both of them held their glass pipes to their lips and put the flame to the top of their stems.

I could hear the rocks sizzle as the flame danced in front of their eyes. The vapors rushed through the glass and they inhaled the fumes. When they exhaled, the smoke filled the air.

How was that Kathy, I asked?

My voice startled her and she quickly put her finger to her mouth and said,

"shhhh, you don't hear that?"

"Hear what," I asked?

When Kathy snapped out her trance she said in a faint voice, "I haven't had a hit like that in years. You feel that shit, Jimmy?"

"Yeah, that shit was good. Y'all got more?"

Kathy raised her hand and released a rock she held in the palm of her hand. Their eyes focused on its descent. After the rock hit the table, Kathy gathered the scattered pieces with a card into two evenly divided piles and asked Jimmy, "which one you want, old man?"

"I told you about that old man shit. Come on out them pants, Jimmy said boldly, and let's do the damn thing."

I ain't thinkin' about your ass Kathy replied, and besides your limp dick ass can't even handle all this."

"Hold up, hold up, Chase interrupted, I ain't come here to see no damn freak show, just smoke and do that shit when we leave."

Jimmy reached on the table to take another hit. Kathy did as well. Once again, the smoke crept up the glass stem to their slightly parted lips. When Kathy put her stem down she began squeezing her breast and making low groaning sounds. Jimmy got up and walked over to the wall unit and opened the cabinet to pull out some VCR tapes. He slid a tape in the VCR and walked back to the couch and waited for the show to begin. By this time Kathy took off her blouse and unzipped her pants. I leaned back in my chair in amazement and waited for the show to begin as well. Both of them.

Chapter Eight

"I'm goin' to the store to get some beer and cigarettes," Chase
yelled. "Niko, you want somethin'?" Yeah, bring me back one of those Bacardi nips. The dark one, alright? "Yeah, I got you." Kathy put in her request and asked, "can I get somethin'?" "You got money, Chase replied, buy your own". "I thought you were treatin'," she questioned. "Yeah aight. What you want?" "A twenty-two ounce bottle of St. Ives. Make sure it's
cold," she added. "You want somethin', Jimmy," Chase asked? "A cold beer would be nice. You need some money?" "Nuh, I got it." "Do you remember the building and apartment number,"

Kathy asked? "We're in the Brisbang building, apartment 11J, right?" "You got it, Kathy confirmed. Just ring the buzzer when

you come back. "Yeah, alright," Chase replied.

Kathy looked over at the remaining crumbs on the table and told Jimmy to "scoop 'em up." She reached in her bra to pull out the last two rocks she had and shook them in her hand like they were dice. She leaned forward towards the table and let the rocks roll out her hand snapping her fingers as though she rolled a seven the hard way.

"I wanna get freaky, Kathy commented. Can y'all handle all this?"

She stood up, put her hands under her breast and lifted them up.

"Damn shorty, you holdin'." I remarked.

"Oh shit," Kathy yelled.

"What's wrong, Kat?" Jimmy questioned.

"Nothin' babe, I thought I lost my shit but, I remembered I put it on the table. You see it Jimmy?"

"Ain't nobody touch your shit, girl. Come on and bring that ass," Jimmy demanded.

"I'm comin', I'm comin', just wait a minute old man."

"I got your old man, hooker," Jimmy replied.

The doorbell rang. Jimmy got up, fixed his robe, and peeked through the peephole.

"Who is it," he asked?

"Tammy. Is Kathy there?"

"Hold up, let me see if she's still here."

Jimmy walked over to the bathroom door and knocked.

"Kathy?"

"Yeah," she yelled.

"Tammy's at the door for you."

"Did you let her in?"

"No."

"Well, let her in asshole."

"Watch your mouth, girl," Jimmy replied.

Jimmy walked back to the door and unlocked it to let the young lady in. Tammy walked inside the apartment scanning for Kathy. Her eyes wide open.

"Hi Jimmy, Tammy said as she continued to scan the apartment. Where's Kat?"

"She'll be right out. She's in the bathroom."

"Could I sit down?" she asked.

"I'm sorry, have a seat baby," Jimmy said politely.

"How you been, Tam?"

"Good, she responded. And you?"

"I'm good, baby. What brings you over?"

She looked over at me, and asked Jimmy, "is it alright to talk?"

"Yeah, he's cool."

"Kathy sold me some good shit and I wanna get some more. Do you know if she still got some left?"

Jimmy looked on the table, pointed to the crumbs scattered about, and said,

"I don't know if that's all she has but she'll be right out."

"Do you mind if I scrap my stem while I wait?" she asked.

"I don't care, Jimmy replied. Do your thing."

She pulled out a paper bag from her pocketbook, sat the bag on her lap and reached inside to pull out its contents. In her hand, she held a stem, a long, skinny metal rod and a lighter. She placed the metal rod inside the glass and began to scrap the insides of the glass.

I leaned over towards Jimmy and asked, "what's she doin'?"

"Scraping the residue from her stem and pushing the screens to the other side," he explained. Without taking her eyes off what she was doing, Tammy asked," you don't get high, do you?" "Nuh, I don't but you go ahead, don't mind me." She continued to scrape the residue from the inside of her stem and then pushed the screens to the other side. Just as she was about to light it, Kathy came out the bathroom with a towel wrapped around her. "Hey girl, what's up?" Kathy greeted?

"I need some of them drugs you had earlier. You still got some?"

"Yeah, but what you see on the table is all I have right now. Can you wait a minute for his partner to come back from the store?"

"Whose partner," Tammy asked?

"Mine," I replied.

"You don't have any on you now?" Tammy asked.

"Nuh, I don't handle that, I explained. My partner will take care of you."

"I don't remember seeing anybody else with y'all when I ran into you guys," Tammy said. "He was holding the elevator. That's why you didn't see him," I replied.

"I wouldn't have remembered anyway, Tammy remarked, I'm blind as a bat without my glasses." She turned to Kathy and asked, "how long he been gone?"

"Not long. He'll be right back. How much you wanna spend?" Kathy asked.

"Forty dollars."

"What you see on the table is all I got right now. You wanna smoke that 'til he gets here?" Tammy leaned forward to examine the two rocks that sat on the table. Kathy sat down on the couch and broke one of the rocks she had and took a piece for herself.

"Is this the same shit Kat?"

"Yeah," she replied.

My beeper went off. I asked Jimmy if I could use his phone.

"Yeah, he said, it's in the kitchen on the wall to the left. You ain't calling long distance, are you?" Nuh, it's a local call.

"Yeah, go ahead."

I walked in the kitchen and picked up the phone. As I was dialing the number, I heard the sound of lighters flicking. I peeked around the wall to watch Tammy and Kathy take their hit and to see what their reactions would be. As I stood there holding the phone waiting for someone to answer, Tammy was taking the flame off her stem and leaned back on the couch.

Someone answered the phone on the other end.

"Who's this?" I asked.

It was Post from 140th and Foch. He called to tell me he needed some more work and Chase wasn't answering his pager.

"How much you got left?" I asked.

Post said he was down to his last twenty pieces and that the smokers were buying pieces like crazy. I'll have Chase call you as soon as he comes back." "How long is that gonna take?" he asked. "Just be patient, I replied, he'll be back in a minute." I had to page Chase to find out where he was. "Jimmy, what's your number so Chase can call me back?"

"718-690-1386 You got it?" Jimmy asked.

"Yeah, I got it."

When I hung up the phone I waited in the kitchen for the phone to ring. Tammy and Kathy sat on opposite ends of the couch with Jimmy in the middle. Once again, Kathy began feeling herself up and Tammy searched through her pocketbook. The buzzer rang. Kathy was startled by the sound. She jumped up from the couch and rushed over to the door to answer it. She pushed the talk button on the intercom and yelled, "Who is it?"

"It's Chase, buzz me in."

"Jimmy you got another robe I can put on?" Kathy asked.

"Yeah, it's in the bedroom."

"Can I get it?" Kathy asked.

"Go ahead, it's behind the door," Jimmy instructed.

Tammy asked Jimmy, while still holding the stem in her hand," you want me to put this up?" "Yeah, put it in your bag for a minute," he replied. As Kathy came out of the bedroom, the doorbell rang.

"I'll get it Jimmy, Kathy said as she walked to the door. Who is it?"

"It's Chase," he said in a loud voice.

Kathy unlocked the door to let him in. When the door opened, he noticed the new face in the apartment and asked, "who's this?"

"I'm Tammy."

"What up?" Chase asked.

"I came to see if I could get some more of them drugs Kathy had earlier. She told me I had to wait 'til you came back from the store. You still holdin'?"

"Yeah, gimme a sec and I'll hook you up."

I told Chase Post called and needed another pack.

"You comin' with me, or are you hangin' out here, "Chase asked.

I'll hang out here 'til you come back. How much product you have on you?, I asked.

"Plenty," Chase said. "I'll leave you what I have and stop by my house to pick up some more, aight?"

Yeah, okay. Make sure you come back to pick me up.

"No doubt, kid."

"Can I have my beer please?" Kathy asked.

"It's in the bag with the rest of the stuff," Chase replied.

I could tell Tammy was getting impatient as she sat on the couch waiting to make her purchase. Chase walked to the door and said, "call me Niko, when you're ready for me to pick you up."

Aight, if I ain't here, I'll be at the shop.

Chase walked out the door. Kathy got up to lock the door behind him and flung off the robe she had on as she walked back to the couch. Her perfectly shaped breast stood at attention as she strolled across the floor wearing a pair of boxer shorts she found in Jimmy's room. Tammy put her forty dollars on the table and asked if she could get two rocks. I opened the bag Chase left to find two nice ones. After I passed her the rocks, she sat down on the couch and prepared her stem to take a quick hit.

"You want some, Jimmy?" Tammy asked.

Immediately, he reached out his hand.

"You don't turn shit down, do you Jimmy? Kathy asked sarcastically.

"Hell no," Jimmy replied.

Kathy leaned back on the couch and waited for Tammy to offer her a piece like she offered her. When she saw Tammy wasn't, she pulled out her stem and scraped the residue that built up from her previous hits.

As she scraped her stem she mumbled to herself. I could tell she was pissed Tammy didn't offer her anything. After Kathy finished pushing the rezz to the top of her stem, she looked over at Tammy and asked, "you don't have a piece for me?"

Tammy was about to put her stem to her mouth to take a hit as Kathy asked her question.

Tammy held up one finger and told Kathy, "just let me take this hit and I got you."

After Tammy took her hit, she slowly lowered her stem and became motionless. Her mouth hung open slightly as drool oozed down her chin. Jimmy tapped her on her shoulder and asked her if she was alright. She seemed as though she couldn't hear a thing he was saying by the way she continued to sit in her trance.

Kathy, still waiting for Tammy to pass her something to smoke, clapped her hands and said, "snap out that shit bitch, and break me off a piece."

Tammy finally snapped out her trance, wiped the drool from her chin with the back of her hand and said, "that's some good shit. I haven't got stuck like that in a along time."

She looked over at Kathy and asked, "did you say something to me a minute ago?"

"Yeah bitch! I asked you to break me off a 'lil somethin'."

"Yeah, yeah, Tammy said. I got you girl. Hold up a minute while I get myself together."

Chapter Nine

Jimmy and I have been working closely with one another for the past two months. He supplies me with credit cards and I make sure he has all the drugs he needs. Everything seems to be going well but, my lady, Casandra, isn't happy at all. The other night I pulled up in the driveway and noticed all the lights were out in the house. I got out my Jeep, walked up the stairs and put my key in the door. I left the door open so I could find my way. I reached for the lamp that usually sat on the table to the right of the entrance. It wasn't there. I walked further into the house and stumbled over some bags that were on the floor. I flicked the living room lights on and saw boxes all around. It looked like we just moved in but, in my gut I felt she was gone. I went upstairs to our bedroom and didn't see her perfumes, make-up, or even her hair care products. I scratched my head trying to figure out what the hell was going on. I walked around to my side of the bed and found an envelope propped up against the telephone. I opened the envelope and read the note. I could almost imagine what she wrote. I unfolded the letter and began to read.

"Niko,

By the time you find this letter, I would've moved most of my stuff out. I'm moving cause I can no longer sit here in this house by myself wondering if tonight you'll come home. I don't know what you're out there doing but I know you're not doing it with me. When I first met you, I told you one of the reasons I wasn't in a relationship. It was because the person I was with paid more attention to the streets and his friends than to me.

I didn't like it then, and I don't like it now. To be in a relationship means we share things with one another. Ever since Ming died, I don't know you anymore. You won't let me help you work through what you're feeling. And I can't stand it anymore. If you're closed to me, then who are you open to? I don't know. Only you and God know the answer to that. I can't like live this anymore. And until you figure out what's more important to you, I feel I need to move on with my life. If that means finding someone who I can share my life with, someone who'll be there for me without question, then, that's what I'll do. Don't get me wrong, I love you with all my heart but I just can't live like this anymore. I pray to God that you find whatever it is you're looking for but for now, I feel you're not interested in being with me and that shit hurts. I would appreciate it if you just left me alone until you figure out what

it is you want in your life. The streets, your friends, or me?
You decide. Whatever it is, I'll always love you and will
continue to pray for you.
Casandra.

After reading her letter, a feeling came over me I
never felt before. Words can't explain it but it felt like
tiny pins were sticking me all over my body and
emptiness filled the pit of my stomach. I leaped to my
feet, rushed downstairs, and flung open the front door. I
walked outside to the curb and looked up and down the
block hoping I would see her.

I walked back in the house and picked up the phone
in the living room to call her mother, thinking maybe she
might've heard from her. When her mother picked up
the phone, I asked her had she seen or heard from
Casandra. She told me she had spoken with her earlier
and thought she was home with me. She asked me was
everything okay and I told her I wasn't sure.

"Is there anything I can do?" she asked.

I don't know, Ms. Sherman. I'll just have to wait
and see if she calls.

"You let me know if you hear from her," she
remarked.

I will Ms. Sherman, I replied, and hung up the
phone.

I sat on the couch for a few minutes, trying to gather
my thoughts but I couldn't. I got up, reached in my
pocket to find my keys, walked outside and got in my
Jeep. I sat there for a while with the motor running and
tried to figure out where Casandra might've gone. My

mind drew a blank. My pager beeped. I looked at the number that came up and went back in the house to call the number. Before I picked up the phone, it rang. I hoped it was Casandra. But it wasn't. It was Chase calling to find out if I was going over to Lafrak City. I told him Casandra had left and he asked if I were alright. I told him I was and that I was gonna stay in the house to see if she called. He asked if I wanted him to come over.

"Nuh, I told him, that's alright, I'll be okay. I'll speak to you in the morning."

I went back out to my Jeep, took it out of park and drove around to the liquor store. John John, the guy that owns the liquor store on 221st Street, noticed as soon as I walked in the door, that something was wrong. "What up Niko?"

Nothin' kid. What's up with you?

"I'm good. What you need young blood?" he asked.

A fifth of E&J.

"You look like you got a lot on your mind tonight. Is everything okay?" he asked.

Yeah, I'm cool.

"Listen kid, you know you can talk with me if you need to."

Nuh, that's alright. I'm good.

"Alright man, come by and see me if you need to," alright?

Yeah, no doubt. I'll come by tomorrow, in the afternoon.

"I'll be looking for ya," he said.

I turned around and walked out the store. One of Casandra's girlfriends, Gail, was coming in as I was going out.

"Hi Niko, where's Casandra?" she asked. I lied and told her she was home. "She didn't leave yet?"

Nuh, why you ask?

"She said she was going to her cousin's house in Jersey for the rest of the weekend."

Oh yeah, she never told me she was going out there, I replied.

"Tell her to give me a call so I can find out if she still wants to hang out with the girls, okay?" Yeah sure, I'll tell her. Have a nice night, I said as I walked back to my Jeep.

I jumped in my Jeep and raced around to the house to find the number to her cousin's house in Jersey. I remembered her name was Cynthia. I got to the house and ran upstairs to find her phone book. It was gone. I tried to remember the number in my head but couldn't. I checked the caller ID to see if the number was there. Anything that had a 201 area code, I called. There were two numbers that had that area code but they were from three days ago. I called the first number.

The phone kept ringing but no one answered. I tried the second number. The phone rang twice before someone picked up. It was a woman.

"Hello, is this Cynthia," I asked politely?

The person on the phone said "no, it's not."

She then asked who was calling. I told her my name and she said I must have the wrong number. I told her I found this number on my caller ID and was returning the call. She asked me what my number was and I gave it to her.

"You know someone by the name of Casandra?" I asked.

"Casandra, sorry, the name doesn't sound familiar," she replied.

Okay, thanks anyway.

I hung up the phone and once again sat on the edge of my bed trying to figure out where she could be. I picked up the phone again and called the first number I dialed. This time, a recording came on.

"Welcome to New Jersey Transit. Press one for bus information and time schedules."

I hung up the phone realizing that the second number must have been Cynthia's. I called the number back. The phone rang about ten times before a recording came on. was hoping the recording would give the person's name but it didn't. All it said was leave a message and someone would call back. I left a message.

If this is Cynthia, I would appreciate it if you would asked Casandra to call me as soon as she could to let me know she's alright. Thanks.

I popped the top of the E&J and took a deep gulp. wasn't use to drinking but, tonight, it really didn't matter.

I don't know which affected me more, the emptiness I felt in my gut, or the burning sensation the liquor had as it heated my insides. My pager went off again. It was Jimmy. I picked up the phone to dial the number. The phone rang once and he picked up.

"Niko, can you come by the house?"

For what? I asked.

"I got some more cards for you, he said. And I need some more of them things you got."

I don't have any product on me. I gotta call Chase and see if he'll drop something off to you. "How long it's gonna take?" he asked.

I don't know. I'll page him after I hang up with you and call you back and let you know what the deal is, okay?

"Yeah, alright. Don't leave me hanging Niko, I ain't got no drugs and I really need some tonight," Jimmy explained.

Why? I asked.

"I ran into this new chick over here that can suck a golf ball through a water hose and she ain't greedy like them other hookers. But, I'm down to my last two rocks and I'm trying to stretch them as best I can. I need you to hurry up, if you can, alright?"

Yeah alright, let me see where Chase is, and I'll call you back.

After I hung up the phone, I thought to myself, maybe I should go over there and hang out with them and relieve some of my stress. The idea began to appeal to me more and more. I paged Chase to see where he was. It didn't take him long to call me back.

Chase, where are you? I asked.

"I'm on 232nd and 137th Avenue at this girl's house, why?"

You got anything on you?

"Yeah, why?"

Jimmy just called and said he has some cards for me. I wanted to go over there, hit his ass off, and snatch them shits up before he does something else with them.

"Aight, what you want me to bring?" Chase asked.

About an ounce.

"No problem. I'll be there in fifteen minutes," he said.

Yeah cool. Call me when you're close.

"You got it Kid. I'll see you in a "lil bit."

He hung up the phone.

I called Jimmy back and told him I'd be there in about an hour or so. Before I hung up, I asked him, who's the girl with you at your house?

"You don't know her, I just met her today."

Keep her there 'til I get there. I wanna see what she looks like.

"Alright, hurry up."

As soon as Chase gets here, I'm out.

"I'll be waiting," Jimmy said.

I looked at the bottle of E&J, which was now half full and took another deep gulp. It went down smoother this time. I took another sip and put the bottle on the dresser and laid back on the bed until Chase called. I dosed off and dreamt about the day I was released from prison.

"Niko, you ready yet? Wilkenson asked. We leave in half an hour. So make sure you got everything you're taking cause we ain't turning around to come back.

Bring your bags to the front and I'll help you bring them to the lobby." Wilkenson was one of the first CO's I met when I got to Gothen. In my dream I saw myself walking down the long hallway of the dorm with all my bags. The whole dorm cheered as if their favorite football team had just scored a major touchdown. Wilkinson, and another staff by the name of Mr. Henry, were waiting for me at the front of the dorm. After shaking hands and slapping five with all the fellas, I stood in the doorway, looked back, and remember what I had gone through and thanked God for bringing me through that shit safely. Wilkenson grabbed a few of the bags I was carrying and told me, "step it up so we can get outta here."

He didn't have to tell me twice. When we got to the first floor, I stopped by the mess hall where I worked for the past three and a half years. As soon as I walked in the door Ms. Bridges was wiping down the counters after breakfast. The first thing she did when she saw me was grab me, gave me a hug and said you take care of yourself and stay out of trouble. She gave me a kiss on the cheek and we said our good-byes. I remembered the farewell dinner the kitchen staff made for me the night before, which consisted of steak, corn on the cob, rice, gravy, and for dessert, a big pan of banana pudding. Ms. B. gave me her number and told me to keep in touch and let her know how I was doing. When I stepped out into the hallway the Director, Mr. Burthoff, a balding, distinguished gentlemen of about fifty or so, was coming down the hall. He was always in a rush but today he stopped to shake my hand and told me, "you keep your nose clean and you'll never have to see a place like this again son. Just do the right thing and you'll be alright."

He turned and went about his business. As we got to the visiting area, Jean Rose, the facility's Athletics Director, was coming in. He spoke briefly with me about my plans for the future and wished me well. Finally, I made it to the front door where the van was waiting. At a quarter to nine, we were on our way to Manhattan where I had to stop to see my parole officer. There wasn't much conversation after we left the facility, just the sound of music playing on the radio and the wheels rolling on the pavement. I sat back and enjoyed the ride and allowed my thoughts to drift back to what had brought me there. Back in seventy-nine, I was arrested for seven counts of armed robbery and was sentenced to three to nine years in a state correctional facility. When I got to Gothen, I hadn't completed high school but was able to get my High School Equivalency Diploma and started taking some liberal arts courses provided by Marist College. I'm proud to say it was because of me and ten other inmates that Gothen Annex started its own college program and helped some of us misdirected youths to achieve more than just a high school diploma. I left there with about sixty college credits and an ambition to continue my education when I got back in the swing of things. My dream shifted to how happy my family would be to have me home again and not visit me under conditions dictated by a correctional facility. I remember how sad my moms looked when the prison guards announced visiting hours were over. They would yell out in a loud and clear voice, "Fifteen minutes to say your good-byes. All inmates walk toward the officers at the rear of the room.

Families remain at your tables and you'll be escorted out as soon as all inmates have been accounted for."

Those sounds would no longer be a part of my reality. I was leaving that life behind me with every mile we passed.

By now, we were getting closer to the city. I could tell because the air no longer smelled clean as it does upstate. In the distance, I could see the tops of skyscrapers. When we got off the expressway, familiar sights and sounds of the city came rushing toward me. Car horns blaring, pedestrians crossing the streets, waves of people on both sides coming from all directions. I almost forgot how crowded and congested the city was. I loved every minute of it. It dawned on me, no matter what, life goes on. I started checking out the passengers in other cars, especially the women.

It's been a long time since I laid eyes on a beautiful woman and the sights made my head spin in every direction. The closest I came to a beautiful woman in the last four years was between the covers of porno books. Women were all over the place and looked good. Nothing could compare to the sights and sounds I was experiencing. For now, my sightseeing tour would have to wait 'cause we pulled up in front of the parole office

on 41st Street between Eight and Ninth Avenue. People were standing in front of the building smoking cigarettes and drinking coffee, holding conversation like they were planning some kind of corporate merger but dressed as though they were ready to stick something up. When I got out of the van, a few of the people standing in front the building acknowledged my arrival with slight head movements. The sight of a person coming home must be a common occurrence for this place. I stepped up to the heavy metal doors that lead me to the lobby of this dingy, depressing building and stopped by the receptionist desk to announce my arrival. I was hoping to see some young chick with a pretty smile and perfectly shaped breasts, direct me to my next destination, but instead, I saw two heavy set black women with badges around their necks who looked at me from above the rims of their glasses. Both looked to be in their late fifties and probably worked for the Division of Parole since the days of Al Capone. Without having to take a second glance, one of the women began to rundown some information that must've been imbedded in her memory from the time she started working there. If you're reporting for the first time, she said, you must go to the eighth floor to meet with the District Supervisor. He'll inform you who you'll be assigned to. The elevators are at the end of the hall. If you're here for any other reason, take a seat and someone will be with you shortly. After being informed of my options, Wilkenson and I turned around and walked towards the elevators. The inside of the elevator looked as bad as the lobby. Poor lighting and the floor tiles were worn out from constant traffic. When the doors to the elevator closed, I pushed the button for the eighth floor. The elevator stopped on every floor but the eight. When we finally reached our destination, we approached a checkpoint to find out who the District Supervisor was and if he was available. A young white guy, who looked to be no more than twenty-five or thirty, was walking past and asked if we were being helped.

I'm Niko Bonds. I just got released and I was told I need to see the District Supervisor.

"What facility were you released from?" the young guy asked.

Gothen Annex, I said.

He looked at me, as if he never heard of the place, and asked,"where's that?"

I told him in Gothen New York, it's a juvenile facility. Another white guy walked up. This guy looked to be in his mid forties, tall with an Archie Bunker kind of look. White hair, fat round face, with his gut hanging over his belt.

He asked the other guy, "what's going on?"

The young guy pointed to me and said, "this guy just got released from Gothen Annex."

The older guy asked the same question, "where the hell is that?"

Wilkenson jumped in the conversation and explained who he was, and where I was released from.

Mr. Bergman, the older white guy, looked back at me and asked, "how old were you when you pulled your first robbery?"

"Fourteen," I said.

"You think you some kind of tough guy or wanna be gangster? Cause if you are, I got something for your ass. Understand?"

Yes sir, I answered.

"Do as you're told for the next two years and I'll be happy with that.

Understand?"

Yes sir, I replied. "Come on, let's see if I can find your P.O."

We stood in the entrance of his office facing a bunch of cubicles. The smell of his stink ass cigar filled my nose. He scanned the area to see if he could find his target. To the left of us, elevator doors opened and four people got off. Two white guys with badges, and a Spanish guy. The Spanish guy had his hands cuffed behind his back. He looked fucked up in the face as though he caught a beat down from one of the officers. The three guys walked past. A short woman officer stepped out from behind the three guys.

"I see you finally caught that asshole, Mr. Bergman said. Where'd you catch him?"

"He took me for a run down a fire escape, through an alley and then for another four blocks before I caught him and tackled his ass to the ground," the little lady said.

With a slight smile on his face, Mr. Bergman asked, "how'd his face get all fucked up?"

The lady officer, who stood no taller than five feet, responded by saying, "I did it. He pissed me off." I started saying to myself, I hope this ain't my P.O. Right then, as if I wasn't even there or he just didn't give two shits whether I heard, Bergman said, "well, here's another asshole for you. He just got released today. He's all yours. Play nice."

He turned and walked back into his office and closed the door. She looked me up and down and said to follow her. Once again we walked through the maze of cubicles. We came to a small sitting area that was half filled with people waiting to see their Parole Officers as well. She pointed to a seat and said, "park it, I'll be right with you."

Wilkenson leaned over to me and asked, "would you fuck her?"

I looked at him like he was crazy. After a moment of thought, I turned to him, with a straight face and said, "right about now I'd fuck a rattlesnake."

From the inside of her cubical, I heard her call for me to enter. She was sitting behind a desk that looked to be too big for her. I imagined the only way she could see over the top of the desk would be to prop herself up on some phone books.

She leaned back in you chair reading my folder. She opened the conversation by telling me her name, which was Anita James. I'll be your P.O. for now but I see you'll be living in Queens so your case will be sent over to our

Queens office. It says here you were convicted of armed robbery. Several counts of it. You like stickin' people up?"

No, I said.

"Who will you be staying with in Queens?"

My moms.

She asked if I had a good relationship with my family.

Yes, I replied.

"Here's the deal, she explained. I'm not a hard person to get along with, you do as you're told and don't give me no shit, report on time, and if you're going to be late, call and let me know. This way I don't have to violate your ass. You have any questions?"

No, I answered.

She told me to report to her in a week and we'll talk about my plans for the future. She stood up from her desk and extended her hand to me. I took notice she didn't look half bad for a white girl. She had a nice smile but all I could imagine was this little woman whipping up on that Spanish guy. Her hand was soft and I could see the shape of her hips through the jeans she wore. She stood with one hand on her waist just above the silver-plated .45 automatic that was tucked in her waist holster. She ended our conversation by saying, "I'll see you next week."

Wilkenson and I turned and walked out of her office. When we got in the van, Wilkenson said to me, "these people don't look like they're fucking around, so I advise you to pay attention and don't fuck up."

Chapter Ten

From the side of the house, I heard Chase calling me.

"Yo Niko! Open the fuckin' door."

His yelling woke me up. I opened my eyes and felt the room spinning. Pushing myself up with my elbow, I sat on the edge of the bed. As I sat there, the room spun faster. My head and stomach battled to see which one would bring me to my knees. I stumbled over to the window, and felt the cool night air blowing against the beads of sweat that formed on my forehead. I stuck my head out the window and saw Chase standing in the driveway.

"Throw the keys down, Chase yelled, so I can let myself in."

Yeah alright, I answered.

I stood up to search through my pockets for the keys. As I rose, the contents of my stomach pushed through my mouth. I lunged forward towards the window so I wouldn't vomit on myself. Chase stepped to his left to escape the rush of fluids. It was like a scene from the Exorcist.

"You nasty motherfucker. You almost caught me, Chase screamed. Brush that dragon out your mouth, he said jokingly, and bring your ass downstairs."

Shut the fuck up, I yelled, I'll be down in a minute. I wobbled backward from the window and made my way towards the hallway stairs. Standing at the top of the stairs, I still felt nauseous but managed to wobble my way down to the front door. As I approached the door, Chase began banging.

Stop bangin' on the fuckin' door, I yelled, I'm here. I opened the door for Chase to enter. No sooner than the door opened, I had to throw up again. I rushed past Chase and headed straight for the side of the house where I made my next deposit. Chase stood off to the side and watched as I spilled my guts.

He started laughing at me while asking, "what the fuck you ate kid, some bad pussy?"

Nuh man, I brought a bottle of liquor and it messed my stomach up.

Chase held his fingers together to form a cross as he spoke to me.

"You need to brush your gums man, your breath smell like straight ass and feet. Damn Niko, is shit that bad?"

What you talkin' about. My girl just left me. What would you do if your girl left you? I asked. "I'd have a fuckin' party and find the next chick, he explained. Listen Niko, I know right now you're feeling kinda fucked up about Casandra leavin' but you need to snap out that shit and get your head together. We got business to take care of, and I need you to be on point. I brought the package you asked me to bring, so get your shit together and let's be out."

Yeah, alright, I replied. Come on inside so I can change my clothes.

I walked upstairs and opened the bathroom door to turn on the shower. My stomach continued to rumble but I didn't have to vomit anymore. I looked at myself in the mirror and saw how bloodshot my eyes were. Chase came upstairs and asked if I needed any help.

Yeah, I told him, look in the closet in the bedroom towards the back and find me a sweat suit to wear. I opened the medicine cabinet to get a tube of toothpaste. Instead, I found the ring I gave Casandra for our engagement. I sat down on the tub, held the ring in my hand, and remembered the night I gave it to her. It was a Thursday night. Casandra had to work late and wouldn't be home until nine. I planned that night from the time we got up that morning. As soon as she walked out the door to go to work, I got dressed and went to the grocery store to buy the food I needed for the evening. I'm not that good of a cook but I did my thing that night. I made Cornish Hens with rice, gravy, steamed broccoli with hot dinner rolls and for dessert, I brought a nice size carrot cake. Her favorite. Around eight-thirty, Casandra called to let me know she was getting in her car to come home. It would take her about twenty minutes to get home. I turned off all the lights in the house, and lit some aroma candles and I sat them on the dining room table. I heard her car pull up, and the car door slam close. She put her key in the front door and walked into the living room.

"What you up to Niko?" Casandra asked.

"I just wanna show you how special you are to me," I replied.

I helped her take off her jacket and walked her into the dining room. I pulled out her chair and she sat down at the head of the table. A cold bottle of Dom Perignon chilled to the right of her. I poured her a glass and walked into the kitchen to bring out the main course. As she sipped her Champagne, the light from the candles reflected off the bubbles that filled her glass. She smiled as I walked into the dining room wearing her apron and carrying our dinner. The look she had on her face let me know she was happy. Before we started eating, I told her how much I loved her and wanted to spend the rest of my life with her.

She leaned forward and gave me a kiss and said she'd like that. I got out my chair and kneeled down beside her. I held her hand in mine and asked her to marry me.

"Niko! What the fuck you doin' man? We gotta go kid. Snap out that shit and get it together," Chase yelled.

You know how to fuck up a good thought, I replied.

"Get your ass in the shower, Chase commanded, so we can get outta here. We're runnin' late. You forgot we gotta go over to Jimmy's house to pick up those cards."

Alright kid, relax I'll be ready in a minute.

I closed the door and got in the shower. As I was washing up, my pager went off. I pulled my pager off my belt and looked at the number. I could hear Chases' pager going off as well. I jumped out the shower and walked into the bedroom. Chase and I looked at each other and said, "something's up."

I asked him what number popped up on his pager.

"718-978-4219," he said.

That's the same number I got. I told him to dial the number and see what's up. He picked up the phone and waited for someone to answer.

"Yeah, who's this?" Chase asked.

He didn't say anything after that but, "un huh, uh huh, yeah alright, we'll be there in a minute," and hung up the phone.

Who was that" I asked.

"That was Post on 140th saying that the police just snatched up the crew over there."

Let's be out, I said.

I threw on my clothes, hurried downstairs, got in Chases' car and raced over to 140th Street. We rolled up on the block, and noticed that no one was out. Chase parked around the corner from where our crew would be. We got out the car and stood across the street. Post came walking up the block from the other direction.

"What's up, Post?" Chase asked.

"Nothin' black."

"What happened out here?" Chase asked.

Post explained he was across the street serving a custie when the boys rolled up from all directions. They got out their cars with their guns drawn and told everybody to get on the ground. They searched through everybody's pockets and stuffed the money they found in their pockets. One cop, Post continued, found that stash wrapped in a paper bag under the back wheel of a parked car. After they found everything they could, they put cuffs on everybody, piled them into a police van, and pulled off.

How many they take? I asked.

"The whole crew," Post said.

As we stood there talking, a patrol car drove past. When they reached the corner, they stopped, backed up and parked in front of us.

"What you guys doin' out here?" one of the cops asked.

We live in the neighborhood, I said.

"You guys holding any drugs?" the cop questioned.

"Nuh officer, we just having a conversation," I replied.

"Where you guys live?" the cop continued.

Two blocks from here, I said.

The other cop got out the patrol car holding the handle of his gun like he was about to pull out on us. The cop sitting in the patrol car asked us to come closer.

When we approached, he had his gun sitting on his lap with hammer pulled back.

"If we search you guys, we won't find anything, will we?" the cop asked.

Immediately I thought about the drugs Chase brought for me and if he had the pack on him. "No, office, Chase said. We ain't got nothin'. What you looking for?"

"Jumbo's, as you guys would say, the cop said sarcastically, I hear you guys got it good over here." "I don't know what you talkin' about officer," Chase said.

"Oh really, the cop standing outside the patrol car said, as he walked around to where we were standing. I hear you're one of the main niggas' out here."

"Officer, I don't have a clue about what you're talking about," Chase said.

"We got pictures of you and your whole crew. You wanna see," the cop in the patrol car asked? He showed us pictures of Chase getting out of his car. Some of the pictures showed him slapping five with one of the brothers' they arrested. Another one showed him passing a bag to the same brother and walking away to get back in his car.

"I should lock your crack selling black ass up right now," the cop said. "For what," Chase asked? All you got are some pictures of a guy that may or may not be me."

"Don't insult my intelligence, the cop said, I know who you are and what you guys are out here doing. It's just a matter of time before I have your ass in handcuffs. I'm surprised you weren't out here earlier.

We would've locked your ass up with the rest of them," the cop said with a smile on his face. "Well officer, Chase said, you gotta do what you gottsa do and so do I. And right about now if y'all ain't arresting us, we got things to take care of. Can we go now," Chase asked?

Yeah, get outta here but if we come back through here and see you guys standing around, we gonna lock your asses up for loitering."

The other cop walked up to Chase's face and said, "when I catch your ass, I'm gonna enjoy putting the cuffs on you. You hear me? Get the fuck off my block and don't let me see you guys around here no more tonight."

Chase stood there, looking straight in the officers eyes, and said, "Officer, you drive safely and have a nice night."

As they were about to pull off, my pager beeped. It was Jimmy. He was calling to find out if I was on my way.

Lets get outta here, I told Chase, and head over to Jimmy's house to get them cards. "Post, where you gonna be later," Chase asked? We'll come back through to drop you off some product if you wanna make some money tonight."

"Y'all ain't got nut'in on y'all now," Post asked?

"Yeah but it's only five hundred dollar's worth, you want that," Chase asked?

"Yeah man, pass that."

Chase told him, "don't worry about that small shit, keep that for yourself and beep me if you hear anything else about our peeps. Aight?"

"Yeah, aight, I'll hit you up later," Post said.

Chase and I walked over to his car and got in. We sat there on the block for a minute and talked about what we should do next.

I suggested we go over to Jimmy's to get those cards and just wait 'til someone from our crew calls to let us know what's going on. Chase agreed. He started the car and drove towards the expressway. We got off at the Junction Avenue exit, and crept though 57th Avenue. Chase pulled into the driveway of the Bisbang building and was approached by a security guard. Chase and I opened our doors and got out the car. The security guard asked him how long we're planning on staying?

"Not long, Chase said. Maybe twenty minutes, tops."

"You cannot park here that long, the security guard said. I'm supposed to report any cars that are parked for more that ten minutes," he explained.

"If I gave you twenty dollars, would you make sure no one messes with my car?"

The security guard looked around to see if anybody was looking, saw the twenty dollars in Chases' hand and quickly grabbed the money. We walked into the lobby of the building and headed for the elevators. As we waited for the elevator, Kathy walked up.

"Hey Niko. What up Chase? Y'all goin' to see Jimmy," she asked?

"Yeah, Chase said, hang out down here for a 'lil while so we can take care of some business first. Come up in about an hour, aight."

"Alright," Kathy replied, as she turned to walk away.

The elevator doors opened. We stepped inside and pressed for the eleventh floor. As we stepped off the elevator, Jimmy opened his apartment door to peek in the hallway.

"Damn Jimmy you must've smelled us coming," Chase said jokingly.

"Nuh, I heard the elevator doors open and figured it might be you guys."

"Come on in, I got somebody I want y'all to meet."

Chase and I stepped inside the apartment and quickly scanned the place to see who was there. "So where's this fine ass chick you were talkin' about," I asked?

"Ain't nobody here with this nigga, Chase said. All that shit was game to get us over here quicker." The bathroom toilet flushed, and the door opened slowly. Chase and I turned to see who would come out. The vision of beauty I saw standing before me was like none I've ever seen. I looked at Chase whose mouth was wide open and saw his eyes scan this woman's body from head to toe. She stepped forward and extended her hand to greet us.

"Hi my name is Tasha. And you are?

I've never seen Chase at a lost for words when it came to speaking to women. He stuttered with his words. Finally, he told her his name.

"Chase, what kinda name is that," Tasha asked curiously as she shook his hand.

"It's just a 'lil sumthin' my boys been callin' me from when we were kids."

"I guess you must be Niko. I've heard a lot about you in the short time I've been here. It's nice to meet you guys'."

Again, she politely extended her hand to greet me. Her red nail polish reflected the light from the lamp.

"Damn Miss Lady, you're absolutely gorgeous," I said.

"Thank you," she replied, while batting her eyelashes and exposing her mesmerizing brown eyes. She stood about five foot five with short, wavy, jet-black hair. Her facial features reminded me of one of those models you see in Essence Magazine. Beautifully glowing, her complexion, a reddish caramel, displayed the look someone would have after lying on the beach in the Bahamas. Her skin was flawless. She stood in front of me wearing a T-shirt that barely concealed a matching set of red undergarments. She led me by the hand over to the couch and sat between Chase and me, with her back slightly turned away from him. That pissed Chase off. Chase likes attention. Especially when it comes to the opposite sex.

"Jimmy, where's the cards," Chase asked in a demanding voice?

"There're in my room."

"Go get 'em so we can see what we working with."

Jimmy jumped up from the couch and rushed into his bedroom to get the cards. As he walked away he said he already activated the cards by ordering some items from the liquor store. He came back into the living room holding two bottles.

"This is what I ordered from the liquor store earlier," Jimmy explained.

"How I know you brought that shit with the cards you about to give us," Chase asked?

"Cause the receipt shows the card number and the date it was used, I replied.

Jimmy ain't stupid. He knows not to fuck up."

"What kinda liquor you bought Jimmy, Tasha asked?

"Actually, I didn't buy liquor. I bought two bottles of Champagne. Dom P and a bottle of Moet. It came out to two hundred thirty five dollars and some change. I used both cards."

"What's the balance on the cards," I asked?

"One card has forty-eight hundred on it, and the other card has thirty-five hundred on it," Jimmy said.

"Can I get paid now," Jimmy asked?

"Be easy, Chase said sternly, gimme a sec. I got you. What you wanna do Niko, you wanna get 'em?" Yeah, pay the brothers.

Chase opened a plastic baggie he had in his hand and poured the contents onto the coffee table in front of us. The boulders he poured out hit the table and bounced around like golf balls, but remained in tact.

"That's for me," Jimmy asked?

His eyes lit up with anticipation as Chase pushed the rocks into one pile. He sat down on the couch, opened the cabinet underneath the coffee table and pulled out his stem. I watched him as he put a wire from an umbrella in the top of the glass and began pushing the screens to the other side.

Why you doin' all that, I asked?

"To make sure there's no hole in my screens and mess my hit up," he explained.

"Tasha you want some of this," Jimmy asked?

"Yeah, I could go for a hit right about now," she replied.

"Ya'll ain't smokin' that shit around me, Chase said, wait 'til I leave."

Jimmy looked at him like he was crazy but kept on fixing his stem to make it just right.

"You leavin' with me Niko?"

Nuh, kid. I'm gonna hang out here tonight. I'll call you in the morning so we can make some moves with these cards.

"You sure man," Chase questioned?

Yeah, I'll be alright.

"If you need me, beep me," Chase said as he stood up to leave.

"You leavin'," Tasha asked?

"Yeah babe but I'll stay if you and I can have a 'lil quiet time together," Chase remarked.

"What kinda quiet time you talkin' about?"

"You know girl, don't act like you don't understand what time it is," Chase replied.

"No I don't understand. If you think I'm one of these chicken headed hookers out here that'll suck your dick for a five-dollar piece, you got the wrong bitch. I don't need you or your drugs. I got my own money and can buy whatever I need honey. So get that shit straight right now. In fact, how much drugs you got on you," Tasha asked?

"You can't afford what I got baby," Chase said sarcastically.

Tasha got up from the couch and walked over to the chair where her clothes were and pulled her Coach pocketbook and pulled out a matching Coach wallet and walked back to where she was sitting.

"Now, Tasha taunted, how much you want to sell, nigga rich?"

Chase looked around and let out a slight laugh and said, "all I got is this big ass rock. You want this?" "How much," Tasha asked with authority? "Gimme two hundred dollars," Chase replied. "No problem," Tasha said, as she opened her wallet and pulled out a roll of crisp hundred-dollar bills. "Damn baby, you holdin' like that, Chase said with a smile on his face. I'm impressed."

"Don't be. Just pass me my shit," Tasha snipped.

"You got it mama. Relax, I'm leavin'."

"You are? I'm sorry you have to leave, Tasha said as she walked Chase to the door. You drive safely and don't' spend all your money in one spot, okay?"

Chase stepped outside the door, and turned to say something. Tasha put her finger to her mouth and told him, "you don't have to say anything, just carry your 'lil ass on home," and slammed the door in his face.

That was cold, I told her, but necessary. He'll be alright.

Tasha walked back over to the couch and sat down right next to me and said, "I'm glad you didn't leave."

Chapter Eleven

Late in the evening I got a beep from Post. When I called him back he told me he had heard from one of the brothers that got locked up.

Post said, the brother was yelling and screaming that somebody needs to bail them out before shit got ugly.

I asked Post, what he means by that?

"You know what that shit means. He's about to drop dime to keep the weight off his ass." He said anything else, I asked?

"Nuh, Post said, just that we better make some moves to get them out."

Tasha was sitting by me as I was talking and began to console me. "Everything will be okay Niko," she whispered.

She asked me if there was anything she could do to help me relax. I asked her if she had any suggestions.

"Yeah, I do, she said. Jimmy, is it alright if Niko and I go in your bedroom for a little while?" "Go ahead, Jimmy said. I'll be right here watching my movies and smoking my shit."

Before we got to the bedroom, the buzzer rang. I heard Jimmy ask who it was and the person on the other end said it's Kathy.

"You comin' up?"

"Yeah, buzz the door," she yelled.

Tasha and I sat on the bed and talked for a while. I asked her to tell me a 'lil something about herself. She began by saying that she was attracted to me and that she would like for us to get to know one another better.

Alright, I said.

"I moved here from Chicago and have been living in the city for the past five years on my own. The reason, she explained, I moved to New York was because I graduated from college with a degree in finance and felt the city would be the best place to find a high paying job. When I got here, most of the companies I interviewed with gave me the impression they were only interested in me being a receptionist and didn't care too much about the skills I had. They just wanted me to be a showpiece in the lobby of their offices. I couldn't take it, she continued, and finally quit to find another job."

While I was looking, I met this guy who I later found out was the CEO of a major corporation. He offered to take care of me until I got on my feet. He made sure my rent was paid and that I always had money. In return, I accompanied him to social events his company sponsored and had sex with him when his wife would act up. He introduced me to some of his rich friends who would call on me whenever they were in town. They would take me out to expensive restaurants, Broadway plays, and pick me up in limos. I didn't mind having to spend the night with them because I'm freaky like that and enjoy a good fuck. Most of the time, I would wear their asses out before they wore me out. The bottom line is, I provided a service for them and they made sure they took good care of me. Last year, I made over seventy thousand dollars. I have a beautiful condo in Harlem and when I feel like it, I jump in my Benz and go wherever the hell I want.

It hasn't been easy being by myself and coming home to an empty apartment. I want a man in my life, she said, and definitely enjoy being pampered by my mate, which I haven't had in quite some time."

My beeper went off again but this time it was Chase. I guess he wanted to know if Post had called. When I called him back, I told him I spoke to Post and that we needed to get together to make a decision about what we were going to do about bailing them brothers' out.

"Let them niggas' handle their business, Chase said. If they have to do some time, oh well, that's the price you pay for being in the game.

You can't do that shit, I told him, we gotta get them brothers out before they create problems for us. I don't give a fuck about them niggas', Chase argued, if you wanna bail them out, go ahead. And besides *BOSS*, it's your call anyway. I told him to come to Lefrak and pick me up at the barbershop. I knew I could easily put my hands on about twenty or thirty thousand dollars without any problems. After I hung up with Chase, I called our attorney, Jonathan Goronsky, and told him what happened. I asked him to meet us at the courthouse in an hour.

"It's gonna cost a lot of money to take care of this situation Mr. Bonds. You need to bring plenty of cash, the attorney continued, so I can get your partners' out tonight."

"Why you gotta go daddy, Tasha asked, why can't you have your partner take care of this so I can spend some time with you. I'm sure if you let me I can take your mind off of all your troubles."

"Listen, I ain't gonna be long, and when I come back we can do whatever you wanna do." I opened the door to the bedroom and startled Jimmy as he was taking a hit. He dropped his stem in his lap and burned the shit out of himself. Tasha laughed as she walked out the room behind me, and asked, "you alright Jimmy?"

"Uh ha, I'm alright," he managed to say, as smoke filled the air.

Tasha walked me to the elevator and got real close up on me and wrapped her arms around me so she could give me a kiss. I pulled back.

"What's the matter, she asked? You don't wanna kiss me daddy?"

It ain't that, I said, I can't get past the idea of the next man's dick being in your mouth. Let's face it, that's what you do."

"Not anymore daddy, I haven't had to do that shit in a long time. I pick and choose whose dick I want in this mouth."

She kissed me on the cheek and asked me to hurry back so she could show me how I made her feel. The elevator doors opened and Kathy walked out.

"What up Niko? Where you goin'?"

I gotta take care of some business. Why?

"Cause I need somethin' to smoke," she said

I don't have anything on me right now, I replied.

"Don't worry I'll take care of that daddy, Tasha remarked, you go on and do what you gotta do so you can hurry back."

Before the elevator doors closed, Tasha leaned in towards me, gave me a kiss on the cheek, and said, "hurry up, daddy, I'm waiting for you."

I got to the shop, took the locks off, pulled up the gate and opened the door to let myself in. I turned on the lights and the TV and walked to my office. Underneath my desk sat a safe that only Chase and I have the combination to.

I opened the safe and counted off thirty thousand dollars and put it in a knapsack I had in the office. While I was waiting for Chase, I decided to trim myself up. Fifteen minutes later Chase tapped on the door with his keys. The expression on his face looked like he was pissed off about something. I opened the door to let him in.

As soon as he walked in, he said, "why we gotta spend all this money to get them niggas' out? Cause it's the right thing to do, I replied. Them niggas' could bring us problems.

"Look here Niko, I know it's the right thing to do, Chase explained, but them niggas' gotta handle that shit and be patient. I don't like partin' with my money kid. That's the shit I'm pissed about."

Stop being a cheap ass ma'fucker, shut the fuck up, and grab the fuckin' bag out the office. We gotta go.

Before I locked up, I asked Chase, do you have anything you need to leave here?

"Oh yeah, Chase remembered, I got my burner on me and a few pieces."

Damn kid, you about to get us locked the fuck up too. Think Chase.

"Yeah, you're right Niko. I'm just pissed right now cause we gotta pay all this fuckin' money out, he explained. I hate that shit."

Chase and I walked to his car, which was parked in the driveway of the Panama building. When we got outside the building, a tow truck was parked in front of his car.

"What the fuck y'all doin', Chase yelled as he ran towards them, I just parked here ten minutes ago." "That's not what the security guards record shows, the tow truck driver reported."

"You gotta be kiddin', Chase replied. Let me see what time he has."

The guy in the tow truck told the security guard to bring him the clipboard that shows the time Chase parked his car.

The security guard, a thin, turban wearing, Indian guy, came from inside the building with his clipboard under his arm.

"Show me the entry for this car," the tow truck driver asked?

"I logged this license plate in at 10:17 pm. It's now 10:31 pm," the security guard explained. "Damn man, for three minutes you gonna tow my car and charge me," Chase asked?

"Sorry sir, its Lefrak City's policy that any car parked in this driveway for more than ten minutes needs to be towed. If you like, I can call my supervisor and see if he'll allow you to pay on the spot so I don't have to tow your car. Would you like me to make the call?"

"How much that gonna cost," Chase asked angrily? If I tow your car to the lot, it'll cost you a hundred twenty dollars to get it out."

"Call the motherfucker, Chase barked, and see what he says."

He was about to pick up the phone when another tow truck pulled into the driveway. I knew the guy driving cause he bring his son into my shop to get his haircut. He jumped out of his truck and walked over to his partner in the other truck. They talked for a minute and came over to us after they finished.

"I'm sorry for the delay sir. My partner didn't know you have the right to park here because you have a business in the building."

"Can we go now," Chase asked?

"Yes sir, just make sure you stop in the security office in the basement of this building to get a parking pass so no one will tow your car in the future," he concluded.

Thanks man, I replied, and shook his hand. The next time you bring your kid into the shop the haircut is on the house.

Chase and I got in the car with the quickness and jetted out the driveway to make it to night court in Kew Gardens, which was about fifteen minutes away. Mr. Goronsky was standing in the front of the courthouse when we pulled up. He didn't even ask how we were doing. All he wanted to know was if we had the money.

"It's in the bag," Chase said as he held up the knapsack.

"Okay, Mr. Goronsky said. Let's go inside and see what's going on."

"We don't get a receipt," Chase questioned?

Shut the fuck up. Where the fuck he gonna go. We'll be right there in the courtroom with him to see every move he makes.

"I still don't trust that cracker Niko, he acts like one of those sheisty ass mafuckers' that always tell you he'll get you off and after you pay him an asshole full of money he fucks around and gets you an asshole full of time."

We walked into the courtroom together but Chase turned right to sit on the other side. Both of us sat in the back and waited for the lawyer to do his thing.

Two For Five

"Up next your Honor, the court officer yelled, docket number Q269714, Q269715, Q2697." The Judge interrupted the court officer.

Enough already, just gimme the damn files.

"Your Honor, the Assistant District Attorney said, the charges are criminal possession of a controlled substance with intent to distribute, and felonious loitering."

"So, in other words, they were standing on a corner selling drugs. Is that what you're telling me counselor," the Judge asked?

"Yes your Honor, said the short, blond haired ADA. Undercover officers made hand-to-hand drug transactions with the defendants in exchange for fifty dollars of United States currency. We ask your Honor to set a bail of ten thousand dollars apiece for the defendants."

"That's kind of steep, the Judge said. What do you have to say about all this defense counsel?" "Your Honor let me first state my name for the record. Jonathan Goronsky, Attorney for the defense. I feel the ADA is missing one important piece of evidence."

"And what's that," asked the gray-haired Judge?

"The drugs! I don't see in the report where drugs were taken off any of my clients. In fact, I don't see where drugs were even found anywhere around my clients. How can you say you purchased drugs and not be able to produce them? Can you answer that Miss District Attorney?"

"Yeah, tell me where the hell the drugs are," asked the Judge?

"Your Honor, the ADA began, from looking at the report, I can't tell whether the officers documented that information."

"What the hell is this counselor, some kinda pre-law bullshit? You know that you don't come into my courtroom without having all your facts together.

On the charges of criminal possession of a controlled substance, the charges are hereby dismissed. With regard to the charges of felonious loitering, let me ask the defendants something. Were you guys hanging out on the corner?"

The whole crew said, "yes sir."

"Then that charge will stand and I'm ordering that bail be set at twenty five hundred dollars apiece for each of you.

If you guys plead guilty to the charges right now, I'll offer you one hundred hours of community service and reduce the charge to a misdemeanor. Take it or leave it. It's your choice."

"We'd like to settle this case now your Honor," Mr. Goronsky replied.

"Okay, your clients will plead guilty to misdemeanor loitering and accept the sentence of one hundred hours of community service," the Judge ordered?

"Yes, your Honor, they plead guilty and are ready for sentencing," Mr. Goronsky responded.

Chase walked over to where I was sitting, and asked," we gotta pay twenty five hundred dollars for each of them *and they still gotta do community service?*"

"Nuh kid, all they gotta do is the community service and the bail is dead."

"What about the money the cops took," Chase asked?

"Forget that. They ain't givin' that shit up, I replied. And besides, we got off real cheap this time. It's time we start changing things around and move our crews off them corners."

"What you talkin' about doin'," Chase asked?

"Maybe we can set up some spots like we got in Lefrak."

Mr. Goronsky stepped back from the Judge's bench, walked to where Chase and I were and told us his fee would be five thousand dollars. Chase took the knapsack from him and walked out the courtroom. Mr. Goronsky followed him out.

As my crew was being led out the courtroom, I noticed that one of the brothers gave a heads up to the officers sitting in the front row. I got up from my seat and caught up with Chase and the attorney.

Chase had given him the money he was suppose to and looked like it broke his heart to part with it. "You guys may need to consider another way of conducting business, especially since it seems the police have targeted your locations and will be looking to do all they can to stop your cash flow."

Chase looked at him like he was about to say something. I pulled him by his arm and lead him away.

"Why you do that, Chase asked? I was about to tell that motherfucker to stick his suggestions up his ass. Just concentrate on being a fuckin' attorney and stop tryin' to tell us how to run our fuckin' business."

He's right," I said. We need to find a new location so the boys don't know what we're doin' and if they get too close, be able to shut shit down with the least amount of losses.

Chase and I left the courthouse and went to the parking lot to pick up his car. We drove back around to the front of the courthouse and waited for our crew to come out. The court officers said they should be processed in about a half-hour or so. As we waited, Chase and I talked about how we could set things up differently so that our operations don't get interrupted again.

"Let's find some crack head that has their own house or apartment, and set up shop there," Chase suggested.

"Yeah, I was thinking the same thing but whose house you talkin' about," I questioned? "Maybe we can put that kid Waters on again, Chase suggested, only this time we'll have one of our people in the house with his ass so he don't rob us like he did before."

Aight, when we get back around the block, let's stop over there and see what's up.

Two of the brothers came out from the courthouse and got in the car with us. Lakim, one of the brothers from our crew, told us he heard Mike, the one I saw giving the officers in the court a heads up, talking to the cops when they were in the precinct. After he talked with them he was put in a cell by himself.

"You don't know what they talked about," Chase asked?

Nuh, cause when the officer came back, Mike wasn't with them. But when we got to the courthouse he was the only one that was able to make a phone call.

Lakim continued to tell us that some of the other brothers were saying that if y'all didn't come bail them out, they were gonna drop dime. Who are the ones that were takin' all that shit, I asked?

"Mike, Shamik, Black. Them niggas'. They were talkin' in the bullpen cause they didn't think y'all were gonna show up.

I kept telling them, Lakim explained, shut the fuck up and handle this shit.

When Mike was put in the cell, before you see the Judge, he told us he had talked to Post and Post told him that y'all would be there to bail us out.

That kinda quieted them niggas' down. And when they saw y'all in the courtroom with the attorney, them niggas' acted like it was the second coming."

Mike came out the courthouse with the rest of the crew and got in the car with the other brothers'. Chase immediately told Mike to get the hell out his car and catch the train. I reached in my pocket to give him some money so he could pay his fare. Chase got out the car as Mike was getting out and walked straight up to his face. "I heard you been runnin' your mouth to the cops. What's that all about?"

"Ain't nobody say shit to them ma'fuckers," Mike replied.

"Then why these brothers' saying when you got to the precinct you were put in a cell by yourself," I asked?

"Cause the cops thought they could get me to rat y'all out," Mike replied.

"I think you bullshittin' us and *did* tell the cops somethin'," Chase said angrily.

"Man, y'all believe what you want. I ain't no snitch," Mike said in his defense.

Outta nowhere, Chase snuffed Mike in the mouth and continued to pound his ass out right in front the courthouse. Me, and two other brothers' had to pull Chase off him. Once we got them separated, Chase walked away from the car but turned back around with some karate move like he was Bruce Lee or some shit. He did a roundhouse kick that caught Mike on the side of his face. Mike fell to the ground and Chase stomped the hell out of his ass again.

When he finished, Chase told Mike," catch the fuckin' train cause if you stayed in my sight I'm gonna pull over every chance I get to whip your ass."

Mike got up, brushed off his clothes and walked off heading towards the subway. The other brothers got in a cab and Chase told them to meet us by Waters' house. I had other plans. I told Chase to drop me back in Lefrak City so I could put the rest of the money back in the safe.

"That's not the only reason you wanna go back to Lefrak, Chase remarked, you wanna go see that hooker waiting for you."

"You got that right," I replied.

After I put the money in the safe I called Jimmy to make sure Tasha was still there. Jimmy said she's been in the bedroom for the past three hours by herself. I asked him to put her on the phone.

"What's up mama?"

"Is this Niko," Tasha asked?

Yeah, I'm on my way.

"Alright, I'll be here."

Aight, I'll see you in a minute.

As I walked over to Jimmy's house, I thought about all the shit that happened tonight and decided I'm gonna chill out, relax, and enjoy Tasha's company.

Chapter Twelve

When I got back to Jimmy's apartment, Jimmy was sitting in the same spot I left him. Only this time his eyes were as big as saucers, and most of the drugs I left him were gone. I asked him where Tasha was. He was so fucked up he couldn't even speak. He just pointed to his bedroom. I pushed open the bedroom door and Tasha was there by herself lying across the bed.

"Hi baby, she greeted, did everything go alright?"

Yeah, everybody got one hundred hours of community service.

"Are you alright? You look kind of tired."

I'm good. What you been doin' since I left?

Stretching out across the bed, she said, and relaxing. You wanna join me?

I sat down on the bed. Tasha got up to help me take off my jacket. I don't know if she was doing it on purpose or if she didn't mind having her breast all up in my face. She looked down at me with a smile as though she was happy to have me there. After she got my jacket off she pushed me back on the bed and laid down next to me.

"Tell me something Niko, you ever met someone you thought would fit well in your life?" Yeah, I did but she's gone.

"Who you talkin' about, *your girl*," Tasha asked curiously?

Yeah, she broke out on me because I was spending too much time in the streets and not enough time with her.

"I know it takes a lot to maintain a relationship, and at the same time, you have to do what you gotta do when it comes to making money. You think she understood that?"

Right now I don't know what to think.

"I can help take your mind off all that for a little while," she said.

How you gonna do that, I asked?

"That depend on you, daddy. What you want me to do," she asked sexily?

What you do best, I questioned?

"Truthfully, just listen. I told you, that part of my life is over. I've made my money and now I do as I damn well please. I travel when I want, see who I want, and don't have to answer to a soul. What I'm looking for right now I'm feeling in you," she continued. The question is, are you feelin' me?"

What you want from me, I questioned?

"I want a man that knows how to handle his business and at the same time, be able to reach out to me to let me know he's thinking about me. I need a man to pamper me and tell me those sweet things you men tell women when y'all want some ass. But not just because you want some, but because you're really feelin' me. I wanna be special to you. In return, I'll do whatever makes you happy," Tasha concluded.

As she was talking, she was massaging my thigh and moving her hand closer and closer towards her goal. She unzipped my pants, pulled up my shirt and played with the

hairs on my stomach.

"You know what else I want Niko, Tasha questioned? "

No, what, I asked?

"I wanna take a hit and taste every part of you," she replied.

Why you need to take a hit first, I asked?

"That shit makes me horny as hell," she explained.

Tasha got up from the bed and looked into the living room where Jimmy was sitting and asked if she could close the door. All I heard faintly was, uh ha, uh ha. Tasha closed the door, sat on the edge of the bed and pulled out an "L" shaped pipe that looked like it was made of brass. She tapped it on the dresser and the screens fell out. She straightened the screens out and put them back in the top of her pipe. From the ashtray, she took some ashes and tapped the top of her pipe to settle the ashes. She laid the pipe down in the ashtray and stuck her hand in her bra. She pulled out a plastic bag and placed it on the nightstand. Tasha turned back to see if I was watching her.

How long you been smokin' that shit, I asked?

Without lifting her eyes from what she was doing, she said, "I've been smoking for over twenty years. Long before they started calling this shit crack. Back then they called it base," she explained.

Don't you ever get tired of wasting your money on that stuff, I asked?

"No, cause I don't get high like that. I smoke because it takes me to a different place in my mind. The average smoker, she explained, wants to smoke crack whenever they can and as much as they can. The problem is, most people tease themselves by buying four or five dimes at a time and when

the night's over they wind up spending three, four hundred dollars on this shit. I don't tease myself. I don't smoke like I'm a broke muffler and I damn sure don't kibble and bit myself." Kibble and bits, what you mean by that, I questioned?

"You know, a person that takes a 'lil piece off a rock and puts it in their stem and then two seconds later puts another small ass piece in.

That shit would drive me crazy. If you gonna smoke, SMOKE!! I've always been able to put this shit down whenever I want to. It never interferes with me taking care of my business. But when I feel like smokin', I'm gonna smoke. Does it bother you that I get high," she asked?

Nuh, do you baby. As long as it don't have you actin' like a fiend, and stealing shit, then do your thing," I said.

She flicked her lighter a couple of times, I guess to make sure it worked properly and put the "L" shaped brass pipe to her lips. She heated the bottom of the pipe and took short puffs. She held the flame to the top of the pipe and took a long pull and put the pipe down in the ashtray. Then she leaned back on the bed and blew the smoke out.

I looked over at her and asked, you alright?

"I'm fine baby. Now I'm ready to smoke *your* pipe."

She asked me to move up on the bed. I positioned myself with a pillow behind my head and watched her pull her T-shirt off. I saw how shapely and curvaceous her body was and couldn't help but reach out to touch her. She removed her bra and her breasts fell perfectly in place. They just stood there. She sat on top of me and looked me in the eyes and asked, "what you want daddy. I want you to tell me how you want me to satisfy you. Tonight is your night daddy and I'm here to make sure you get all you want."

I told her to take my boots off and help me with my pants. She turned around with her ass pointed in the air and untied my boots. The shape of her ass was unbelievable. No stretch marks, dents, or bruises. Her ass was perfectly shaped. reached out to touch her and felt how soft and squeezable she felt.

She gyrated her backside as I touched her with both hands. I heard the first boot hit the floor. Tasha looked back at me and licked her lips.

"You ready daddy," she asked in an inviting voice.

No doubt. Handle your business girl.

Tasha jumped off the bed and snatched my other boot off. Then she started pulling my pants off. When she removed all the material that blocked her access, she crept her way up towards my erection. She was about to take me in her mouth when Jimmy knocked on the door.

"I'm sorry y'all, Jimmy yelled, you got anything left Tasha? I just smoked my last piece."

"Wait a minute. I'll bring it to you," she replied.

Before she got up, she kissed the tip of my erection and said, "don't move, I'll be right back." She dismounted me and opened the bedroom door. My pager beeped as she left the room. The number on it looked familiar. I picked up the phone and dialed the number. The phone rang four times before somebody answered.

Hello, who's this, I asked?

It was Post. He told me that I should come over to Waters' house as soon as possible cause Mike and Chase were getting ready to set it off.

Chase can handle himself, I said, and if he needs me he'll call me. Where's Mike, I asked?

"He's in the front of the house with a couple of other guys sittin' on Chase's car. Chase already told him if he didn't leave, Post continued, shit was gonna pop off.

Is Chase still in Waters' house right now, I questioned?

"Yeah, Chase and Waters were talking about runnin' some work through this spot when Mike knocked on the door asking for Chase. Chase told him to wait a minute and he'll come out to talk to him. Mike left for a 'lil while but came back with these other kids. I don't know Niko, shit don't look right. What you want me to do," Post asked?

You strapped, I asked?

"No doubt kid" Post said confidently.

Then hold my man down 'till I get there. I'm on my way.

As I hung up the phone, Tasha came back in the room and closed the door. I told her, I got to take care of some business across town."

"How you getting there," she asked?

I'll call a cab. My car is on the other side of town, I explained.

"You don't have to do that, Tasha said, my car is in the parking lot on Junction Boulevard." She looked in her pocketbook for her keys and asked, "how long you gonna be *this* time? I don't know, but I'll be back, I replied.

"How about if I came with you," Tasha asked? "I don't care. Put your clothes on and let's be out." Tasha opened the bedroom door and asked Jimmy if he had anywhere to go cause she was gonna ride with me.

"No, I ain't goin' nowhere. Take your time and y'all be careful out there," he added.

Tasha got dressed and fixed her hair in a ponytail.

"Lets go daddy," she said leading the way to the front door.

When we got to the parking lot, I was impressed at the kind of ride she had.

A fire red Mercedes Benz coupe with tinted windows and white leather interior. She opened the passenger's door and got in.

I turned on the engine and she leaned over to kiss me on the cheek.

"You're gonna kiss me the way I want you to before this night is over Niko, that's for damn sure, you hear me," Tasha concluded?

I hear you. Lets just get to where we gotta go and we'll talk about that later, I replied.

"Go head daddy, I'm in your hands now."

While we were on the expressway, my pager went off again. At the end of the number 911 appeared twice. We got off on the Rockaway Boulevard exit and stopped at a payphone. The number rang about ten times but no one answered. I got back in the car and drove to 140th and Foch to see if I saw anybody outside the store on the corner. No one was there. We made our way down towards 138th Street and saw a crowd of people standing in the street. We crept up the block. I noticed that Chase's car wasn't parked in front of Waters' house. I pulled over to park and told Tasha to stay in the car 'till I got back. Walking through the crowd, I bumped into Post. He told me Chase and Mike were arguing in front of Waters' house.

"Chase told him to go on home before he laced his ass. Mike and this other cat I never seen before, walked up on Chase. The other cat, Post explained, had his hand in his jacket as if he was holdin'. Chase told them both to back up and go on about their business. They didn't listen. Chase walked over to his car to put his key in the door and the other kid walked in between the cars behind Chase and pulled out a gun. Chase ducked and pulled out his gun and got off six shots. Three hit the other guy and one hit Mike in the chest.

Chase walked over to where Mike was lying and let off another four shots. Where you see them lying, is where he left them," Post said.

Which way did Chase go, I asked?

"I don't know, Post replied, he just jumped in his car and sped off."

My pager went off again. It was Chases' number. I walked back to Tasha's car to drive to the nearest payphone. I called Chases' house but no one answered. I paged him twice and left my pager number and house number so he'll know it's me. Tasha and I drove to my house. When we pulled up to the house, there were a couple of boxes sitting on the curb and a cab parked in front with the trunk open. The front door to the house was open. Casandra was inside. I got out the car and told Tasha to sit tight, I'll be right back. As I walked in the house, Casandra was coming down the stairs.

"How you doin' Niko," Casandra asked?

"I'm good."

"I guess you got the note I left you. Why does it smell like that upstairs," she questioned? "I threw up last night and forgot to clean it up," I replied.

"What were you doin' that made you throw up?"

Listen mama, I need to know what the hell's going on with you. You just break out on me like this. What the fucks going on, I asked?

"Niko, for months you've been hanging out 'till all hours of the night leaving me here in this house by myself. I can't take this shit any more. Until you decide what you want to do with yourself, please leave me alone. I love you but I can't do this no more. I don't know from one minute to the next if you're coming home or if you're dead some fuckin' where.

You don't call me like you use to and that shits pissing me off. You have to decide what's more important to you, the streets or me."

As she was speaking the phone rang. I rushed to answer it. It was Chase.

What the fuck happened man?

Chase told me the same thing Post said. He said that Mike had come to Waters' house beefin' about how he treated him in front of the courthouse. Chase said he kept telling Mike to go on home before he got hurt but Mike wouldn't listen.

Where are you now, I asked?

"I'm by the Sunrise Mall in front of the Sears Store," he replied.

Wait right there, I told him, I'm coming to pick you up.

I hung up the phone and turned to Casandra and asked her to stay until I came back.

"Why should I Niko, you just gonna have me sittin here, like always, waiting for your sorry ass to come home. I can't do it. My cab is waiting outside and I gotta go," she said angrily.

Where you goin' so I can call you later, I asked?

"Stay here with me and lets' work this out," Casandra asked.

I can't baby, Chase is in trouble and I need to get to him before the cops do.

"Your relationship is in trouble Niko, but I don't see you goin' out your way to save that. What the fuck you think, I'm gonna keep waitin' for your ass? I'm not, she screamed. I met someone who treats me like a queen and he's always there when I need him. Can you do that?"

Do What, I asked?

"Be there for me like I need you to be," Casandra asked?

Don't I make sure you have all that you need Casandra? Have you ever known me to sleep around, I asked? I'm out here doin' my thing so we can have the things we want.

"You don't get it do you Niko, I just want you baby. I know you're out there doing your thing. You give me anything I ask for but all I need is you to be here with me. Loving me and not out there runnin' the streets like that's all that matters to you."

Listen mama, I gotta go pick up Chase and put him somewhere safe. Can you wait here for a half an hour? If we can't work this out, I'll take you wherever the fuck you wanna go.

"I don't feel I should have to wait Niko. You go ahead and see about Chase. He needs you right now,

Casandra said. If I'm here when you come back, we'll talk. But I ain't promising you nothin', understand?" I was about to walk out the door when Tasha came in the house and called my name. Casandra looked at me and asked, "who's this, *your new bitch?*"

"I'm Miss Bitch to you, Tasha replied, and I just wanted to know if everything was alright with Niko."

"Could you step out my house, Casandra asked, and wait at the curb with the rest of the trash. He'll be out in a minute.

Casandra turned to me and asked, "you want me to believe

you ain't sleepin' around Niko?" What you talkin' about Casandra, she's a friend of mine." "Friend my ass nigga. That bitch got that look." What look you talkin' about, I asked? "Look Niko, you go on and do as you damn well please cause I can't do this no more. If I'm here when you get back fine. If not, you take care of yourself and have fun with your *new friend.*"

Chapter Thirteen

Tasha and I pulled up in front of the Sears Store. Chase was waiting there like he said he would be. Tasha opened her door to let him in.

"What I'm gonna do about my car," Chase questioned? "Did you take everything out of it," Tasha asked? "Yeah," Chase replied. "Then forget that car, Tasha suggested, and let's get you
somewhere where you'll be safe." We can't go back to my house, I commented, cause I'm
sure the cops will be looking there. "We can go to my apartment uptown," Tasha suggested. "You sure," Chase asked? "It's not a problem. At least you'll be cool for a couple of

days until we figure out what to do next," she concluded.

"I'm sorry for acting like an asshole the other day, Chase mentioned, I was kinda fucked up cause you brushed me off like you did, he explained. I definitely appreciate you putting' me up. I won't be there long."

I got some people down south that you can stay with until we figure this shit out. I'll call them tonight, I explained. I'll buy you a bus ticket so you can get up outta here as soon as they give me the okay.

"That shit wasn't my fault Niko, I kept telling that bitch ass nigga to carry his ass on home but he wouldn't listen. When I saw his partner come from around the car with his hand in his jacket, I knew I had to do them niggas' or they'd do me," Chase explained.

"What were you guy's arguing about anyway," Tasha asked?

"The shit that happened in front the courthouse. He said I dissed him in front of his boys. I guess he was tryin' to show them he ain't no punk and could handle his own. Niko, you know me, I wouldn't fuck with a nigga unless he had it coming, Chase commented, he just wouldn't go about his business. I kept tellin' him to let that shit go. Why the fuck couldn't he just fuckin' listen."

Aight, Chase, aight. That shits behind us. Get your head together and forget that shit. I need you to listen to me, aight. Tonight we'll stay at Tasha's. I'll call my people and find out if they can put you up for a 'lil while. Tomorrow morning, your ass is on the first thing smoking out the city, you heard. How much drugs you got at your house, I asked?

"Not that much, Chase replied. About three hundred dollars worth I bagged up yesterday. The rest is in the safe at the barbershop on Foch."

I'll go over there to pick up whatever's there and pass it out to our crews. Don't worry, I assured, I'll take care of everything.

"I'm sorry man for all this shit," Chase said apologetically.

You my man and when I needed you and Ming, y'all were right there. So forget that shit. We gonna get through this like we always do.

"You know Niko, you been tellin' me that ever since Ming died. You've been right. We've been through a lot you and I. I didn't want this to go down like this Niko. I really didn't."

I know kid. But you had to do what you had to do, right?

We pulled up in front of Tasha's apartment building on 135th and Lenox Avenue and were greeted by the doorman.

"Good evening Miss Drake, the doorman said, how are you this evening?"

"Fine thank you. I'm gonna leave the car here for a minute but I'll be back to move it, okay?" "No problem Miss Drake. Take all the time you need."

We walked through the lobby and into a huge elevator. Tasha pressed for the fourteenth floor. The hallway on her floor was decorated with brightly colored plants and well polished floors. Her apartment was at the end of the hallway. She put the key in the door and the lights came on as we entered. The apartment was gorgeous. From her balcony, I could see the city's skyline clearly. The living room was decked out with soft beige leather furniture that matched the parquet floors. The dining room was arranged in an Oriental style. The centerpiece on the table was a large bouquet of yellow roses.

"Make yourselves at home guys, Tasha said, I'll be right out."

Tasha stepped into her bedroom and closed the door behind her. A minute later she opened the door and motioned for me to come in. She was standing behind the door as I entered the room and closed the door slowly behind me. turned around and noticed she had changed into a black, see through nightie that showed her perfectly shaped body. She wrapped her arms around me and wrestled me to the bed. I didn't have a chance to fight her off. She stuck her tongue so far down my throat, I almost gagged.

"I told you you're gonna kiss me the way I want you to before the day was over," Tasha said in an arousing voice.

I stopped resisting and grabbed a handful of her ass and opened my mouth to give her my tongue. She readily sucked on it like it was a piece of tasty candy.

"Take all your clothes off, Tasha ordered, and give mama what she's been waitin' for."

She unbuttoned my shirt and knelt down to untie my boots. I didn't have to do anything. She stripped me naked in two minutes flat. Tasha stood in front of me and slowly took off her nightie. Her eyes focused on me as I laid in her bed fully exposed. She walked around to the other side of her bed and opened the nightstand draw and pulled out a bottle of flavored oil, stood in front of me, turned the bottle upside down, and rubbed the oil on my skin. She got on top of me and pressed her body against mine. Tasha slid her way down to my mid-section and used her tongue to taste every part of my strawberry flavored body.

"You like that daddy," she asked?

I leaned my head back, closed my eyes and let her do whatever she desired.

I could feel her tongue teasing my erection. In one gulp, she took half of me in her mouth. She moaned as she slowly came up.

Come here mama, I demanded, get your pretty ass on top of me.

Tasha slid me inside of her and bounced up and down until she reached her climax.

"Damn daddy, Tasha said in an exhausted tone, I haven't cum like that in years. I knew I was right when I first laid eyes on you."

Right about what, I asked?

"That you would give me all I needed, "she replied.

Chase knocked on the door and asked, "y'all finished in there? A niggas' out here starvin'. Can I fix somethin'' to eat?"

Two For Five

"Yeah sure, Tasha yelled, look in the refrigerator and take whatever you want."

After we finished getting our groove on, Tasha asked me to go downstairs and move the car. "Not only do I need you to move the car, but I need you to drive back to Queens and get them drugs out the safe in your office before the cops do. Oh, and Niko, you might want to go by your house and check on your girl." Damn, I forgot all about her. She's gonna be pissed. "No she's not, Tasha said calmly. Just explain to her you had to see about your man and make sure he's alright. I'm sure she'll understand. If she don't, Tasha concluded, you can always come back home to me." I made it out to Queens and stopped at the shop. For a Sunday night, the shop was packed. I walked to my office, closed the door behind me and opened the safe. Inside were two big plastic bags of coke. One was uncooked, and the other had boulders of crack. Underneath the plastic bags were four stacks of one hundred-dollar bills. I put everything in a plastic garbage bag and walked out the shop. I opened the door on the drivers' side and put the plastic bag on the floor behind the front seat. Now it was time to deal with Casandra. When I pulled up to the corner of my block, I saw Casandra coming out the house and walking towards a car. It didn't look like a cab. A guy was holding the trunk open as she brought box after box out of the house. As she placed the boxes on the ground, he loaded them in the trunk. I sat there on the corner until she finished putting the boxes in the trunk. I watched her get in the front seat of the car and drive off. I followed them. They turned onto Merrick Boulevard and headed for Springfield Boulevard. I guess they were getting on the expressway. I was right. I continued to follow them until they came to a red light on Atlantic Avenue. It was there I made my move.

I pulled up along side of them. I knew they couldn't see me because the windows were tinted. I watched as she leaned in close to him so she could give him a kiss. That shit had me heated. When the light turned green, I pulled off in front of them and slammed on the brakes. He ran into the back of Tasha's car. I pulled my hood over my head before I got out the car so she wouldn't know it was me. He got out his car and walked towards me.

"Hey man, I'm sorry I hit the back of ...."

That's all the words he said. I two pieced his ass dead in the mouth. He fell backwards holding his face. Casandra got out the car and ran to his rescue. I took off my hood. She froze, with her mouth wide open.

"Niko why are you dong this," she questioned.

I didn't say a word. I walked up to him and unleashed all my anger. While he was on the ground, I stomped him repeatedly in the face. Casandra started yelling and screaming for help. As he was sprawled on the ground bleeding, I looked up at her. She could see the anger in my eyes along with the hurt.

Tears formed in my eyes but I refused to let one drop.

"Why, Niko, why," Casandra asked repeatedly."

I still didn't say a word. I kept looking at her and finally turned around and walked away. "I don't ever want to see you again," Casandra yelled.

I turned back around and kicked the guy in his mouth and watched as he spit out his teeth. I got back in Tasha's car and drove off. I didn't have a clue as to where I was heading. I just drove. I came to a red light and a tear rolled down my face.

I pulled over to the side of the street and began thinking about what I just did. I shouldn't have done that. It wasn't his fault my relationship was falling apart. It was mine.

I'm not the kind of person that would lash out at anyone but I couldn't hit her nor would I ever. I got on the expressway and made my way over to Tasha's house. I pulled up in the driveway and got out the car. The doorman came out the building and asked who I was there to see. I told him, Tasha Drake.

"Is she expecting you," he asked?

Yeah, just ring her bell and let her know that Niko is here.

He called her to let her know I was there.

"Let him up, "Tasha replied over the intercom.

"You know you can't leave your car parked here too long, the doorman commented?

Yeah I know. I'll be back in five minutes to move it.

When the elevator opened on Tasha's floor, she was waiting by the door for me. She could see in my eyes something was wrong.

"What's the matter Niko?"

Nothing, I replied.

"Why you lying to me?"

I don't feel like talkin' about it right now.

"Come on in the house and sit down," Tasha ordered.

When we got in her apartment, Chase was knocked out on the couch. Tasha pulled me by the arm into her bedroom and closed the door. She put her hands on my shoulder and asked me again.

"Tell me what happened. Did you see her," she asked?

I still refused to say anything. I just sat there looking at the floor.

"Niko, you got to tell me what's wrong. If something happened, then tell me."

A tear fell from my eye. She turned my face towards hers and wiped the tear away.

"You don't have to say anything, she said, I know that look. You ran into her, didn't you?" Yeah, I replied, with someone else.

"That shit must've hurt, Tasha remarked, but at least now you know what's up with her. It's going to take a minute for that feeling to go away but I'll be here for you when you need. You can count on that," Tasha assured.

"Where you park the car," she asked?

In front of the building. I had an accident, I explained.

"What kind of accident," Tasha asked?

"A car hit me from behind."

"Did you get the license plate number," Tasha asked?

Nuh, cause it was the car Casandra was in.

"Explain to me how that happened," Tasha asked? I pulled out in front of them and slammed on the brakes and he rear-ended me. There's about forty thousand dollars in a bag on the floor behind the front seat, along with two big bags of coke. Go downstairs, I said, and bring that stuff up here.

She got up from the bed and put on her housecoat. Before she walked out the bedroom, she said, "daddy, I ain't worried about the car. We can always get that fixed. I just hope you'll allow me to be there for you. I told you earlier, whatever you need me to do, I'll do."

Chase got up as Tasha walked out the apartment. He came into the bedroom and sat down on the bed beside me.

"I heard you talkin' to Tasha about runnin' into Cssandra. You alright kid?"

"Yeah, I'm alright. Casandra was with this new kid, I explained, and I broke his ass up in front of her." "Damn Kid, now we both got problems," Chase commented.

"Why you say that," I asked?

"Casandra ain't gonna let you get away with that shit."

She ain't gonna call the cops on me.

"I don't know Niko, Chase replied, you should've let that shit go."

Tasha brought the package up from downstairs and sat it on the bed.

"What you guys talkin' about?"

Just goin' over the shits that's been happenin' for the past few days, I explained.

"Y'all got a lot to figure out, Tasha remarked.

"Yeah, and the first thing is, we gotta keep our business up and runnin'," Chase said.

I was thinking about that and I decided we need to get our people off them corners so the cops don't fuck with them. How did things go over at Waters' house, I asked?

"He was interested in our proposition and wanted to know when he could get started."

He still smoking, I asked?

"Not really, Chase said, he still gets high but all I saw him do was smoke weed.

Tasha got in the conversation and said she would do whatever needed to be done if we needed her help. Thanks baby, I know I could count on you. Chase got up and walked into the living room. I heard the refrigerator door open and close. Tasha asked me if I wanted to talk about what happened with Casandra. I told her maybe later we'll talk about it, but right now, I just needed her close to me.

Tasha moved the two plastic bags off the bed and placed them in her closet.

"Do you mind if I take a hit and get undressed.

Do you mama, I replied.

Again, she pulled out that "L" shaped brass pipe and fixed the screens and put them back in the top of her pipe. She reached in her bra and pulled out the plastic bag she had stashed and took out a nice size rock. She broke off a big piece and put it in her pipe. As she took a pull, I rubbed on her breast. She liked that shit. I could tell by the way she lunged forward as I touched her. When she finished taking her hit, she put the pipe down on the nightstand and got up to take off her clothes.

"I'm ready daddy, Tasha said in a provocative voice. I got you right where I want you." She walked over to the other side of the bed to get the flavored oil she had earlier. The look in her eyes turned me on. She put the oil on the table and began helping me take off my clothes.

"I want to see all of you daddy, she commented, take all that shit off and let me do you like you never been done before."

I knew I was in for the ride of my life when she said that. Truth be told, I needed to let go of some of the tension I was feeling.

Tasha got up on the bed and knelt down beside me. She picked up the flavored oil and poured it on us both and told me to lick it off her breast. I did so without hesitation.

Casandra wasn't freaky like Tasha and Tasha enjoyed every moment of it. Even more so, after she took a hit. She got on top of me with her ass in my face and grabbed my erection tightly and began making circular motions around the tip of it with her tongue. I massaged her ass checks with both hands and told her to put it in her mouth. She did with no questions asked. Then she stopped and sat up on my chest, reached over to the nightstand and put another piece in her pipe. She looked back at me and asked if I wanted to try some while she gave me some head.

Yeah, pass that, I told her.

She turned around to show me how to smoke it.

"Put the flame underneath the pipe to let the rock melt a little. Then, she explained, take short pulls so the smoke can build up in the pipe." She moved my hand to the top of the pipe and told me to pull hard and take a deep toke.

Tasha slid down and took me in her mouth. When I took the flame off, I held the smoke in and let the drugs take effect. I felt lifted. That shit was the best feeling I felt in my life. Aside from bussin' a nut.

"You alright daddy," Tasha asked?

Uh ha, is all I could say.

Tasha continued to handle her business and at the same time, she looked me in my eyes to make sure I didn't zone out on her. She stopped for a second and asked me again, "you alright?"

Yeah babe, I'm good.

I never felt like that before and wanted to feel that feeling again. I asked her to put another piece in the pipe for me. She looked at me hesitantly.

What's that look all about, I asked?

"Nothing daddy, I just don't want to get you fucked up off this shit."

Mama, I can handle this shit with no problem, I assured her.

"Yeah alright, she said, I've seen motherfuckers get twisted off this shit. So, take it easy daddy. You don't have to rush. Just enjoy it for a 'lil while and then take another hit."

I wanna rock right now, I ordered, put me another piece in here and let's get back to where we were.

Chapter Fourteen

The next morning I got up, walked into the living room and

saw Chase sitting up watching TV.

What up kid? Did you get any sleep?

"A little, Chase replied, I kept thinking about what happened last night. You know the cops gonna be all over our operation. That shits gonna be a pain in the ass, Chase continued. I didn't want shit to be like this Niko."

I told you last night, don't worry about it. I'll take care of this. And besides, you need a vacation anyway, I said jokingly.

"Yeah but, not like this.. I'm gonna be on the run for the rest of my life.

That's fucked up kid."

"Tasha told me last night, she knows this lawyer that helps brothers get outta shit."

"Yeah, what's up with him," Chase questioned?

"I don't know, she didn't go into details. When she gets up we'll ask her to get in touch with him. Right now all I need you to do is lay low until I have a chance to find out more information, alright."

"Yeah, I guess I'll have to," Chase replied.

As we were talking, Tasha got up to go to the bathroom. She stopped for a minute to say good morning, and kept walking. When she finished in the bathroom, she came over to the couch and asked Chase how he was holding up.

"I'm not feelin' this runnin' shit," Chase explained. "I know it's gonna be kinda rough, Tasha remarked, but you gotta give Niko and me a chance to work this out."

"I know a few people that can pull some strings for me if I asked them to," Tasha said confidently. "Like who," Chase asked?

"I have a friend that's a lawyer, Tasha explained, he works for this big time law firm on Wall Street. He's the best at what he does. Only thing, he's real expensive."

How expensive, I asked?

I don't care how much that shit cost, Chase said boldly. "Hire his ass."

"All I gotta do is call him and let him know what the deal is, Tasha assured. I'm sure he'll work something out for me."

Work something out, what you mean by that, I asked?

"Do I gotta fuck him? Is that what you're asking? That shit ain't happening, Tasha stated. In fact, that motherfucker *owes* me. He told me, anytime I need his help, call him."

"When you gonna call him," Chase questioned?

"It's too early to call him now, Tasha replied. He usually don't get to work 'til ten or eleven." Alright, what we need to do, I explained, is get a bus ticket for your ass.

"I ain't goin' nowhere until I know y'all got this lawyer guy in play," Chase stated. What you think, you gonna hang out here 'til we hire him, I asked?

"It shouldn't take long to find out what's up with this guy, will it?"

"I don't know, Tasha answered. But what I do know is Niko will be able to move a lot easier if he knows you're safe."

I already called my man down south and he said you can come down there and chill 'til I have a chance to straighten this thing out.

"Where he lives," Chase asked?

Gainesville.

"Gainesville, Chase questioned, where the hell is that?"

North Carolina, I replied.

"Before you go, I need to set up a meeting with our crew so we can decide who's gonna handle the shit you use to do. You think Post can handle that," I asked?

"Yeah, he's alright. He'll work out fine," Chase replied.

Y'all get dressed so we can get things moving.

While Chase and Tasha were changing, I called all the brothers and told them to meet us at the shop in two hours. The ones I wasn't able to reach, I told the others to make sure they got word to them. I also called Big Ras to make sure he'll be there as well. I'll need him to handle some other business I'm sure will need to be dealt with later. Me, Tasha, and Chase pulled up in front of the shop on Foch Boulevard and got out the car. A group of brothers were in front the shop talking and smoking cigarettes. Inside, the rest of the crew mingled and watched TV. When Chase walked in, the noise stopped and all eyes were on him.

"What y'all looking at," Chase asked?

"Ain't nothing black, one of the brothers said. We heard the cops snatched your ass up yesterday. You alright?"

"No doubt," Chase replied.

I turned off the TV and called the other brothers inside so we could get the meeting started. Everybody that was standing in front the shop piled in and stood wherever they could.

Listen up, I yelled, we need to make some changes and I need you guys to pay attention to what I'm about to say. From now on Post will be my right hand man. He'll make sure all you brothers out there slingin' are well supplied. As I was about to continue, one of the brothers asked, "Niko, those corners are getting hot as hell to work on, what you gonna do about that?" I decided we gonna move our operations indoors, I explained, and use our pagers more to conduct business. If you know a crack head has their own house or apartment, and can easily be influenced to let us run work outta their place, then set that shit up and let me know. Until then, drive around the neighborhood and pass out your pager numbers and let the smokers reach out to you.

"Kinda like a crack delivery service," one of the brothers said jokingly.

In fact, I said, you're right. That's what this is gonna be. A ma'fucker pages you and leaves their number, you call them back and find out where they are. Once you know what they want, the rest is simple. Just deliver the package. The first place we gonna run work out of is Waters' house. Post, I need you to set up teams to work out of that spot. I want two people outside watching who's movin around at all times. Pay close attention to the "boys" slidin' through the block. We don't want attention drawn to our location. The late night hours are different. Around that time, ain't nobody out but smokers anyway. But during the day, STAY ON POINT!

For the most part, things are running the way they should. I'd like to keep it like that. We've been real lucky when it comes to not getting our spots shut down completely. But we need to do things a 'lil different. That's why I'm telling you brothers you need to be on point.

Two For Five

When we open up this spot in Waters' house, we need to follow some simple rules so things will continue to run smooth. The first thing is never underestimate a ma'fucker that smokes. That's because they always schemin' to get the next one. And if you're the herb that they get, that shit's on you. Make sure you keep the pack on you always. Second, if a ma'fucker ain't smokin', they gotta go. Don't allow no beggin' ass ma'fuckas in. That'll keep paying custies from coming back."

After I gave out my instructions, I told everybody that Chase would be off the set for a while and I needed them to handle their part so we could get that money and bring him back home as quickly as possible. Everybody told Chase to keep his head up and exchanged a few hugs and said their parting words. Most of the crew stepped outside to stand in front of the shop.

Chase did as well. I was called into the back office to answer a phone call. It was Big Ras calling to let me know he was on his way. Before I could hang up the phone I heard the sound of a motorcycle in the distance and then gunshots. I dropped the phone and ran to the front with my gun in my hand. Three of my crew lay bleeding on the ground. I looked to see if I saw Chase but didn't. A number of people came from across the street and were looking down at the ground. I walked around to the other side of the parked car and saw Chase sitting against it holding his neck and gagging for air.

I knelt down next to him, took my jacket off and applied pressure to his wound. He was shot twice. Once in the arm and once in the neck. Chase grabbed me by the arm and looked me straight in the eyes and slowly let go. Six police cars rolled up and moved the crowd back on the sidewalk. I remained in the street holding my man in my arms and refused to let go. His blood soaked the sleeves of my shirt.

Two minutes later, an ambulance pulled up. I watched them as they tried to resuscitate him. The EMS workers put him on a stretcher and rolled him into the back of the ambulance. At the hospital, the police said they caught some guy on his motorcycle trying to toss the Tec-9 he used. I later found out the shooter was Mike's older brother. Tasha came to the hospital to wait with me. We sat in the waiting area for hours and still hadn't found out any news about how Chase was doing. I got a page from Post. When I called him back he told me that Chase's girl, Tonya, had been by the shop and heard about Chase getting shot and was on her way to the hospital. I still hadn't called his mother to let her know what happened.

"You know you have to make that call Niko," Tasha said somberly.

Yeah, I know but how am I gonna explain this shit to his moms, I asked?

About an hour or so later, a doctor came out wearing a surgical uniform and asked if we were the patient's family members?

"There's good news and bad news, the doctor said. First, he lost a lot of blood but we were able to extract the bullets in his throat and arm. Second thing, because of the damage the bullet caused to his throat, he probably won't be able to talk.

We're still determining the actual extent of his wounds and felt he was too weak to continue operating. We'll monitor his condition over the next few hours and make a determination as to when to operate again. For the most part, there's nothing we can do but wait. I'll have an update for you in a few hours," the doctor concluded.

Tasha and I fell asleep in the waiting area and woke up to the sounds of a women announcing over the PA system a code blue in the Emergency room. Tasha leaned her head back against the wall and continued to get some rest.

I got up to go to the nurse's station to find out if any new developments had come up. The nurse, a short Jamaican lady, said that he's still in ICU and the doctors are monitoring his progress.

"Go on downstairs, the nurse said, and get yourself a cup of coffee."

She concluded, "pray, child, pray."

I got Tasha up and we both went downstairs to the cafeteria to get something to eat. We sat by the window and watched the sunrise over the tops of buildings.

"You alright Niko," Tasha asked?

I don't know what I feel right now. It's like I'm numb. I still have to call his moms and let her know what's going on, I explained.

"Why don't you do it now, Tasha said, I'll be right by your side baby. I'll help you speak to her."

From the time I met Tasha, she's been a source of encouragement and support. Not once has she asked me for anything but my time. I started thinking about the condition of my life. I came to the conclusion that the choice I've made to make this fast money hustling on the streets, has a price to it. I can't lose any more of my people, I thought. But I can't allow this situation to overwhelm me. I have to stay focused on what needs to be done. Finally, I picked up the phone and called Chase's mother. The phone rang a couple of times and a soft voice answered.

"Praise the Lord," she answered.

"Miss Dawson, this is Niko."

"Clarence is not here baby and I would appreciate it if you told him to call me," she commented. "Miss Dawson, I don't know how to tell you this, but Chase, I mean Clarence was shot yesterday." The phone dropped. I could hear her in the background screaming and crying saying my baby, not my baby, dear Lord please let him be alright. She called me every name under the sun. I never knew she could cuss like that.

"I know it was your fault this happened to Clarence. I kept telling him, she continued, he needs to keep his narrow ass off them streets selling that poison. It's your fault Niko."

Those were the words she left me with. In the waiting area, Tonya sat. As soon as she saw me she slapped me in the face and said damn near the same thing Chase's mother said. I couldn't take it anymore.

Tasha looked in my face and saw how hurt I was. She grabbed me by the arm and told me to come on. We're getting outta here for a little while.

"We'll come back later," she said.

The first liquor store she saw she pulled over to get a bottle of liquor. When she came back to the car she pulled out a big bottle of Hennessey and poured me a cup. Before I knew it, we were in front of her building and the doorman was opening the car door. We got upstairs and she led me straight to the bedroom. She put two cups on the nightstand and poured me some more liquor. Then she opened her nightstand draw and pulled out her brass pipe and sat it on top of the nightstand. She didn't have to ask me if I wanted any, I just helped myself. I chopped off a big piece of rock and stuffed it in the top of the pipe.

"Damn Niko, you can't smoke all that in one shot," Tasha screamed.

Watch me, I said defiantly.

I snatched the lighter out of her hand and puffed on the pipe the way she showed me. I blew the smoke out and the first thing that came to mind was Chase and the fact that I might lose another one of my boys. Tasha looked over at me amazed that I wasn't bugging out from the hit I just took.

"Most people, Tasha said, would've gotten stuck after taking a hit like that. I've seen people actually dive under beds thinking someone was after them just from taking a *small* hit, she continued. But you, damn, you act like this shit don't even phase you."

I reached over to take another piece and Tasha grabbed my hand.

"Niko stop, what you tryin' to do, kill yourself," she asked?

Nuh baby, I just don't wanna feel what I'm feelin' right now," I replied.

"Okay baby, but please take it easy," Tasha said calmly.

Smoke rose from the pipe as I put it down on the nightstand. I leaned back against the headboard and closed my eyes. I felt Tasha's hands rubbing my leg.

"What you thinking about baby," she asked?

About Chase, I replied.

"He's gonna be alright honey, Tasha assured me. You just gotta believe that."

My pager beeped. I checked the number but didn't recognize it. I called the number. It was Casandra. "I heard about Chase, she said sympathetically. How's he doing?"

I don't know yet.

"How you doing," she asked?

I'm not doing too good right now."

"Is there somewhere I could meet you," she asked?

Why, I asked?

"Even though we got our problems, I still love you Niko. I wanna be there to support you, she said. You don't have to go through this by yourself. I'm here for you honey."

Tasha must've figured it was Casandra I was speaking to cause she started doing things to distract my attention. She got on the floor in between my legs and unzipped my pants. I pushed her hand away but she kept fucking with me.

I don't know if I could meet you tonight but in the morning I'll be at the hospital. Maybe you could meet me there, I said.

"Alright, if you need to talk to me, I'm at my mother's house."

Why you over there, I asked?

"That's where I've always been Niko."

Then who was the guy you were with the other day?

"That's a friend of mine from work. He was helping me take some things to this storage company over on Atlantic Avenue," she explained.

I saw you kiss him.

"He likes me but I ain't feelin' him like that Niko. What you think, Casandra asked, I don't love you? All I ever wanted was for you to be with me and not out there doing God knows what, to God knows who.

Look what happened to your partner. I don't want that to happen to you Niko. Don't you understand," she questioned?

Tasha took a rock and put it in her pipe then put it to my lips as Casandra was talking to me. I took a pull. "You listening to me Niko," Casandra asked? I had to blow the smoke out before I answered her. I struggled to sound normal but it didn't come out the way I wanted.

"What you doin'," Casandra asked?

Nothin', I replied.

Tasha put my erection in her mouth as I was talking on the phone and was looking at me as she slowly pleased me. She reached over to pick up her pipe and motioned for me to put another piece in. I did.

"Do you like that daddy," Tasha asked in a low voice?

Casandra heard Tasha's question, and asked, "Am I interrupting you? Call me when you're done Niko," and hung up the phone.

Tasha passed me the lighter and pushed me back against the bed and took me in her mouth as I took another hit. I never felt that kinda feeling before in my life.

Once again, Tasha looked up at me and asked," you like that daddy?"

Uh ha, I groaned.

I thought about Jimmy and how he sounded after he took a good one.

Thoughts came from all direction. I thought about Chase and what his mother said to me.

Then my thoughts shifted to Casandra and whether she was telling me the truth about that guy just being a co-worker. My erection slowly died down to limpness. I pushed Tasha off me and reached for the pipe again.

There were no more drugs on the nightstand. I asked Tasha where's the plastic bag that had the drugs in it. She got up and brought it to me. I opened it, took out a rock the size of a golf ball and smashed it on the nightstand. Tasha sat on the floor in front of me and said you gonna kill yourself smokin' all that Niko. I didn't care at that point.

All I wanted was another hit. Tasha got up and closed the door behind her. I sat in her room for a couple of hours just smoking and thinking about what was going on. When Tasha finally came back in the room, she looked on the nightstand and saw that most of the drugs were gone.

"Niko I don't like what you're doing to yourself and want you to put that shit down and relax," she demanded.

Alright, I told her, just leave me alone for a minute.

"Don't you wanna go back to the hospital to find out if everything is alright with Chase?" Yeah, but not right now, I replied.

"I can't sit around and watch you do this to yourself," Tasha said.

She stormed out the room. I began feeling paranoid and thought that someone was watching me. I got up to look out the window. Even though Tasha's apartment was on the fourteenth floor, I still felt like someone was watching me. I took another hit. When I blew the smoke out, I got up from the bed and walked into the living room. Tasha wasn't there. I searched the apartment. I opened every door in the apartment. I even looked behind the couch thinking I wasn't alone. Sweat poured off my face and my heart was beating a hundred miles a minute. In my hand, I held the brass pipe tightly. It had become my source of comfort and kept me num from feeling. On the kitchen table were Tasha's car keys. I left them there, walked out the apartment and waited for the elevator. When the doors opened, there were five or six people on it. I must've looked weird because everyone on the elevator stared at me like I had two heads or something. Sweat continued to roll off my forehead. The way my heart was pounding I knew without questions that everyone could hear it.

I got off the elevator and walked from 130th Street and Lenox to 130th Street and Fifth Avenue. At the corner, I ran into this young chick, who looked to be about twenty or so. She asked me if I had some change. I asked her what she needed it for. She told me to get something to eat. I could tell she was lying. I asked her if she got high. She said yes.

"Do you know a place where we could go to smoke?"

"Yeah, she said, its right up the block."

She took me to an apartment building on 130th Street and Park Avenue and introduced me to this guy named Jeff. He had an apartment on the first floor. As soon as I walked in the door, I gave him a nice size rock. I asked him if he had a room where I could be alone. We moved from the entrance of the apartment into the living room. Since I didn't see anybody else in the apartment, I figured he was there by himself. The girl, whose name I didn't remember, led the way to the room. Being new to this side of the crack game, I wasn't ready for the barrage of questions this chick had.

"Are you from around here," she asked?

Nuh, I replied.

"Where were you headin' when I ran into you," she questioned?

Nowhere in particular.

She was starting to annoy me with all the questions she was asking. I asked her if she wanted to take a hit.

"Yeah sure," she said with anticipation.

Before I left Tasha's house, I wrapped two golf ball size rocks in paper towel and put the paper towel in a small brown paper bag. When I pulled out the paper towel and showed her the rocks, her eyes got wide as hell.

"Is that crack," she asked?

"Yeah," I replied.

"You ain't kiddin', she commented, you came to smoke."

Chapter Fifteen

Two days have past, and I still haven't gotten any sleep. I've been back and forth to the hospital checking on Chase. His condition hasn't changed. In fact, the other day the doctors told me they didn't think he was going to make it through the night. After a change in the medication they were giving him, he eventually pulled out. Everyday they shoot him up with morphine to control the pain. He opens his eyes and stares at me, but he can't say anything. Tears formed in his eyes and I didn't know what to do to help him, except be by his side. Earlier during the day, his mother and sister were at the hospital and told me they didn't want me to be there while they were there. That shit hurt. They're making it seem as though I was the cause of Chase getting shot. I wasn't. It was one of those things you don't expect to happen. But it did. Sometimes, when I'm alone, I ask myself if I could've done anything to prevent that shit from happening. If I told him to wait for me at Tasha's until I got back from the meeting, maybe he wouldn't be in the condition he's in now. But I know Chase. He wouldn't listened to me anyway. He wouldn't stay in Tasha's apartment by himself. I know that. So why is it that I feel like I had something to do with him getting shot?

Maybe it's because I should've protected him more than I did. I don't know what I'm gonna do if I lose another one of my boys. I've been in contact with Post who told me things are running smoothly at Waters' house and that I need to keep them well supplied because smokers are beating down the door to buy our shit. Fiends love us. Not only do we have the biggest and the best shit out, but we're open all day and all night. Tasha's been paging me constantly. I haven't returned her calls because I'm not in the mood to talk.

Casandra's pissed off with me, so I know not to call her. The only things of interest to me right now are Chase and getting high. Getting high is the only way I can keep my thought from haunting me. I drove by Waters' house to see if everything was going as well as Post said it was. I knocked on the door and Waters answered.

"What up Niko," Waters asked?
Ain nothing' kid. How you?"

"I'm good, he replied. What's going on with Chase?"

He's still holdin' on, I replied.

Post was sitting in the living room playing Nintendo. He got up to give me the money he collected from last night.

"Shits been movin' real nice Niko, Post commented. The first night, we made over three thousand dollars."

What's up with Waters, I asked?

"What you mean," Post questioned?

Is he cool with the arrangement we made with him?

"Yeah he's cool. I make sure he don't run out of drugs, and he stays in his room and let's us do our thing out here."

What about the brothers on the streets, I asked, they staying on point?

"No doubt," Post said.

It seems like you got shit locked down over here. If you need me, beep me.

"How's Chase doing", Post inquired?

He's still in ICU and they haven't given me any new information.

"Yo kid, let me know if he needs anything."

Yeah alright, I said, as I walked out the door.

Before I got to my Jeep, my pager went off. It was Tasha. I called her from a pay phone.

"Where are you Niko?"

In Queens.

"When you comin' to see me," she asked? I don't know right now.

"I miss you Niko."

For a moment I didn't say anything.

"Did you hear me Niko," she asked?

Yeah I heard you.

"So what's wrong, you don't miss me?"

It's not that, I explained, I got a lot on my mind right now.

"Come on home baby, and let's figure this out."

I got a couple of things to take care of. As soon as I'm finished, I'll be there.

"You sure," she questioned?

Yeah, I'm sure.

I was on the corner of Rockaway Boulevard and 137th Avenue. As I walked back to my Jeep, a patrol car drove past me real slow. The officers stared at me. I stared back. I remembered one of them from the other day when Chase got shot. Before I got in my Jeep, they pulled over, got out their patrol car and asked me to put my hands on top of their car. I did. They searched through my pockets and found the money

Post had given me.

"Where you get all this money," one of the officers asked?

I work.

"What kinda job pays you with a bunch of singles," the officer inquired?

The singles, I explained, are for gambling. I play poker.

"I remember you from a few days ago, one of the cops recalled, when I stopped you and two other guys over by the store on Foch and 140th . You don't remember my face?"

No officer, I replied, you must have me mixed up with someone else.

"No, I'm sure it was you and the other guy you were with, I believe his street name is Chase. Is that right," the officer asked?

I didn't answer.

"We know you and a few of your "*brothers*" are out here movin' drugs. And I'm gonna tell you a little secret, the officer whispered. We about to shut your whole

operation down. We know all about the spot on 138th, on Merrick Boulevard, *and* the spots in Lefrak City. We're about to bring your drug selling ass down," the officer remarked.

He was so close I could smell the stale coffee and cigarettes on his breath. They handcuffed me and put me in the back of the patrol car. On the way to the 105th precinct, the officers taunted me by saying things about Chase.

"I heard your partners fucked up and can't talk. How's he gonna "holla" at the girls," the officer joked.

"I'm sure he's gonna miss smoking his "weed", his partner commented.

You know you can't smoke that shit with a hole in your throat, don't you?"

Fuck y'all, I said.

They both laughed.

"You know if you keep doing the shit you're doin', the officer sitting on the passengers side said, you're gonna wind up like your friend, in the hospital or in the morgue. Is that what you want?"

I continued looking out the window and didn't answer them. I knew they didn't have anything on me so I wasn't worried. When we got to the precinct, the Desk Sergeant looked down at me from his desk and said, "I've seen you somewhere before.

You probably saw his picture among the ones we took of that street crew on Foch and 140th, one of the officers replied.

Oh yeah, I remember, I knew I saw your face somewhere before. What's his charge," the Desk Sergeant asked?

"Aside from being an asshole, the officer commented, we picked him up for a busted headlight."

"That's all, the Desk Sergeant questioned? You couldn't find anything in his car?

"No Serg, the officers replied. He wasn't in his car when we picked him up."

"Take him down to lock up and run his prints. If he has warrants, take him over to central booking and let them deal with him."

"Even if you don't have warrants, the officers standing by me whispered, it was good just handcuffing your black ass." I sat in the bullpen for three hours before they came back to tell me I didn't have warrants. I need to make a phone call. Is that possible, I asked?

"When we're finished, the officer said, I'll let you make your call."

How much more you gotta do, I asked?

"Not much more, the officer replied, just sit tight. The detectives wanna have a word with you." Not long after he said that, two detectives stood at my cell.

"My name is Detective O'Hara. I'm in charge of the Tactical Narcotics Task Force here in Queens. My team, he explained, has been monitoring your organization's movements. We know all the players. Clarence Dawson, aka Chase, who's in the hospital fighting for his life, and your other partner, who's now deceased, Harvel Johnson, also known as Ming, have been under investigation by our squad for a long time. We know all about the locations you're currently selling drugs from. We know about the apartments in Lefrak

City, the crew you got on the corners of 228th Street and Merrick, *and* the spot you guys just opened on 138th Street and Foch.

What I'd like to do, the detective continued, is give you a chance to help yourself out."

How's that, I asked?

"We need more information. We need to know if Clarence Dawson was the shooter of those two guys on 138th."

I don't know what you're talking about, I replied.

The detective threw an envelope on the table and told me to open it. Inside were a number of pictures of

Chase, Ming, and our whole crew coming in, or going out of, the barbershop on Foch. They even had pictures of me picking up money from the brothers on the streets.

You got all this information, I said, why you need me?

"Actually, the other detective said, we don't need you. We're giving you a chance to take some of the weight off your shoulders."

Thanks, I said, but no thanks. Can I call my attorney?

"Yeah," the detectives said.

A uniformed officer opened my cell and let me make a call. I called Mr. Goronsky. He told me he would be there shortly to get me out.

The uniformed officer was listening to my conversation.

When I got off the phone the officer said "you should make a deal cause shits about to get real ugly."

Maybe he's the one that gave them all their information. The uniformed officer walked me back to my cell. The detectives continued to detain me and ask questions. Then they stepped out the room. When they returned, one of the detectives said "we're gonna keep you in custody until we sort out some details."

What kinda details, I asked?

"We'll get back to you in a little while," the detective said.

Two more hours passed. My attorney finally showed up and was told, due to an ongoing investigation, they were holding me 'til they gathered all the facts.

"If you're not formally charging my client, Mr. Goronsky said, I want my client released and any further communications you need to have with him you'll do through me."

The detectives turned their backs to talk amongst themselves.

They turned around and said "he can go, but we need to be able to put our hands on him whenever we need to. So don't go anywhere," the detective concluded.

They gave me my property. My beeper had been on all the time I was in lock up. I missed ten beeps. Mr. Goronsky drove me back to my Jeep.

The cops hadn't searched it. I got on the phone and returned all the calls I missed. The first call was to one of my workers in Lefrak City.

He told me that security busted down the door to the apartment and arrested a couple of the brothers. That was the first situation. Next, I called my boys on 228th and Merrick Boulevard and found out that the police had been over there and arrested everyone that was out there hustling. The next call I made was to Casandra. She told me she couldn't go through this with me anymore, and that she made a decision to be with someone else. I figured it might be the guy I saw her with the first time. I hung up. I called the next number. It was Tasha. She was bitching and crying about me not wanting to be with her. I told her she had to understand that right now too many things are going on for me to focus my attention on being with her.

The next call was the call that hurt the most. It was Tonya, Chase's girl.

What's up Tonya?

"Chase died last night," she explained.

My heart dropped. I couldn't speak. She called my name continuously until I answered.

"Did you hear me Niko?"

Tears formed in my eyes. Everything was coming at me all at once. My first thought; take a hit. After I hung up the phone, I got in my Jeep and drove someplace secluded. I turned off the engine, pulled out my pipe, pulled the paper bag out from under my seat and loaded my pipe. I took a deep pull and held the smoke. As I blew it out, I thought about Chase and Ming, my boys. I felt alone and empty. Everything I had was gone. I can't begin to explain all the feelings I felt. As long as I kept smoking, I wouldn't feel this shit. So I thought.

How wrong I was. The thought of Chase dying hit me harder than expected. I couldn't smoke enough to kill that feeling.

I got so paranoid, I left from where I was parked and drove over towards my house in Laurelton. I was about to turn the corner when one of the young kids that lives on my block ran up to my Jeep and told me the police had broke down the door to my house and were still there. I backed up and drove over to the shop on 140th Street. Everywhere I turned my spots were being raided. There were ten to fifteen cop cars on the block in front of the shop and all the people that were in the shop were against the wall in handcuffs. The cops had yellow tape cordoning off the area. The last place I could go was to Tasha's. When I got there she welcomed me in and told me she heard Chase died.

"How you doin' daddy?"

I'll be alright, I replied.

"You look like you need some sleep," Tasha commented.

I haven't been to sleep in a few days.

"Take your jacket off and relax." You

got any drugs here, I asked?

"No Niko, Tasha said sternly, and I aint getting' none for you either."

Listen, I ain't tyrin' to hear all that, I yelled, just get me something to smoke." "No, she said defiantly. You wanna smoke, you go out there and get it yourself."

I got up and walked to the door.

"If you walk out that door Niko, don't bother to come back," Tasha declared.

I turned around and told her, you ain't gotta worry about that.

I didn't know where the hell I was going after she said that, but I damn sure didn't feel like hearing a bunch of bullshit from *anybody*.

The only other place I knew to go was over in Laurelton. There's this abandon house that sits on a hill that's been there for as long as I can remember. No one ever goes in there and I thought that would be a good place to hold up and chill for a minute. Before I got there, I passed by this chick hanging out on the block and asked her if she knew somewhere to get drugs from. She looked at me for a minute and asked, "what you want?"

I need an eight ball.

"Damn papa, you havin' a party," she asked?

Nah, I replied.

"We gotta get to 228th and Merrick and see if them boys are out there on the corner."

I knew where she was talking about. That was one of my spots.

"I think they got busted."

"That shit don't mean nothin', she said. They're usually right back out there in a matter of hours" I told her to get in the Jeep. We pulled up on the block and some young kid I never saw before walked up to the passenger's side and asked what we wanted. "I need some weight," she told the young kid. "How much you want," he asked?

"Gimme all you got," I yelled.

"Wait here, I'll be right back."

The kid jumped on his bike and headed up the street. When he came back, he had another guy with him who asked us who we usually bought from. When he looked in the Jeep, he saw my face.

"You're Niko, right? I heard about you. I was out here the other night when the boys came through. They snatched up everybody, he said. Why you out here looking for drugs?"

"I got some business to take care of. Can you hook me up," I asked?

"Definitely, but listen, I need you to put me on cause ain't nobody out here and people are runnin' looking for shit," he concluded.

"I'll see what I can do," I replied.

I took the Jeep out of park and drove back to the abandon house on 224th and 135th Avenue. I parked around the corner from the house and walked to the back to find a window to climb in. The window on the second floor looked like it was open. I climbed up a tree, jumped on the roof, slid the window up and climbed through. Downstairs didn't look like it was in bad shape. There was a blue leather couch sitting by a window and a television sat on top of an old floor model TV. I switched on the lights. They came on. The girl I was with waited for me in the back of the house. I opened the door so she could come in.

"Is this your house," she asked?

"Nuh, but I know the owner."

"Now that we're here, what's the deal," she asked? I wasn't even thinking about doing anything with this chick, but now that she mentioned it. "I thought we'd smoke first and do a 'lil somethin' later, alright."

"What you talking about doing", she questioned?

"Let's take a hit first and we'll talk about that later."

She sat on the couch and pulled out a metal pipe that looked like an antenna from a TV set. "What's that," I asked?

"It's my stem," she said.

"How long you been smokin' outta that?"

"This shit works better than anything", she explained. "You just gotta know how to use it." I passed her a rock and she took a hit. When I took mine, I couldn't enjoy it because of all the things going on in my head. She noticed that.

"What's wrong," she asked?

"Ain't nothin' babe. A lot of shit's happenin' around me."

"You wanna talk about it?"

"Nah, not really." That's why I'm smokin', cause I don't want to deal with it right now."

"It can't be that bad," she said.

"If you only knew," I replied.

I took another hit and felt that paranoid feeling again. I got up from the couch and walked over towards the window. I pulled the sheet back that covered the window and stared outside. I thought about what Chase's mother said to me. I was the cause of him getting shot. Maybe she was right. Maybe if I told him more forcefully to wait until I got back, he'd still be here.

"Are you alright," the girl asked?

"Yeah, I'll be alright. By the way, what's your name?"

"Shayla. But my friends call me Shae."

"A partner of mine, I explained, once asked me, do I ever feel like just saying fuck it sometimes? That's how I feel right now."

"Why," she asked?

"Cause I know shit ain't gonna get any better," I replied.

"What's going on that has you thinkin' like that?

She started sounding like a psychiatrist with all the questions she was asking. But I didn't mine answering her. I needed to. It helped get some of that stuff out my system.

"Are you in trouble," she asked?

"Yeah", I told her.

"What kinda trouble?"

Before I answered, I took another hit.

"I've been home for less than a year and all hell seems to be breaking loose. I lost two of my best friends, my girl, and whatever chance I had at doing something with my life, I explained. I know they gonna take my businesses and whatever money I got, that's gonna be gone soon too."

"You sound like you gotta lot on your plate, she commented, but I'm gonna tell you something. Shits gotta get better. I know that because I used to be in college not too long ago. I've been smokin' crack for the past ten years, off and on. But I always believed things would change when I allowed them to. You feel me? I can't do anything about the problem I had yesterday or even begin to solve all the problems I have today *but* I can prepare myself to deal with whatever comes tomorrow," she concluded.

That made sense to me.

Chapter Sixteen

Shae stayed with me all night. We talked about everything. She kept me from bugging out. I was down to my last few rocks and didn't have any money left. I needed to come up with an idea to get some more money for drugs. I knew I couldn't go to my house, even if I had money there. I'm sure the cops would've been there already. My next thought was to go to the Laundromat on Hollis Avenue and see if I could get some money from there. I asked Shae if she wanted to take a ride with me.

"Yeah, you don't think I'm gonna sit here by myself, do you?"

"I guess not, I replied. Come on, let's get outta here and make this move."

When we got to the Laundromat the gates were pulled down. The United States Marshals placed a piece of paper on the front gate that said the property had been confiscated. I left from there and went to the barbershop we owned up the street. The same note appeared. I got back in my Jeep and thought about what to do next. I called Mr. Goronsky to find out what was going on. The receptionist said he couldn't come to the phone. Shit's starting to look critical. After I hung up, I called Jimmy. I figured he might have some credit cards I could use. No one answered. I decided to drive over to Lefrak City to see if I could catch up with him. On the way there I stopped by the barbershop on Foch to see if the cops had closed that shop as well. Again, I saw the same note that was on the other stores. I got back on the highway and drove over to Lefrak City. When I pulled into the driveway, Kathy was walking out of Jimmy's building. I asked her if she had seen him.

"You ain't heard," she asked?

"Heard what?"

"Jimmy got fired from his job, she explained, and nobody's seen him since. I just left his house and nobody answered the door."

"Alright, I'll see if I can find out some information from his co-workers at the post office."

I drove around to the post office on Junction Boulevard and ran into one of the postal workers hanging out in front and asked if he had seen Jimmy. He told me the same thing Kathy told me. He got fired for suspicion of credit card theft. I hope he didn't run his mouth about who he gave those cards to. That would be all I need. I ran out of ideas. I didn't have a clue what to do next.

"I got an idea," Shae said.

"Like what", I asked?

"It's gonna involve you and me going up in a grocery store and doing some shopping", she explained?

"What you talkin' about, stealing?"

"Something like that", she replied.

"I ain't with that."

"All we gotta do, she explained, is go in the store like we shopping, you know, like normal people, and get all the stuff we want. Then, she continued, we'll find a friendly cashier and hold a conversation with her while she's ringing up our groceries. While she's doing that, I'll pass you my pocketbook while you're bagging up the groceries. When you get the cart filled up, you just roll the cart out the door to the car. Because of the fact you'll have my pocketbook, the cashier will remind me that you have my pocketbook and tell me to get the money to pay for the groceries.

By that time, you should have the car started and ready to get us the hell outta there", she concluded. "Are you out your fuckin' mind, I asked? That shit won't work."

"Yes it will, she said confidently. I know it will cause I already tried it. The only difference is I'm not using a cab this time. The last time, the cab driver drove off with the food I took cause I had to get out to see what was taking my partner so long. Now we gotta car. It's up to you, she said. I already know who'll buy all the stuff we get and they'll pay straight cash."

I didn't have any other choice. Especially since I was broke. We drove to Key Food on Junction Boulevard, parked the car in the parking lot and gathered our thoughts.

"Don't be nervous, she said, just follow my lead. Act like we a couple. People won't suspect a thing if we act normal."

"I'm not nervous" I replied.

Deep down I didn't like the idea of having to do this. But I knew if I didn't, we wouldn't have any money. We got out the car and walked into the store. The security guard greeted us as we passed him. Shae grabbed a cart and headed straight for the meat section. She piled all kinds of meats in the cart.

"We need some miscellaneous items, she said, to make it look good."

"Like what", I asked?

"You know, things you would normally buy when you go shopping. Get cereal, vegetables, and sodas. Stuff like that", she explained.

I felt real uncomfortable but I kept shopping. When we got to the checkout, she started a conversation with the cashier.

"Hi, how you feelin' today", Shae asked?

"Fine thank you", the short acne faced white girl replied.

"My boyfriend doesn't want me to go over five hundred dollars. Could you let me know when you reach that amount?"

"Sure", the cashier replied.

"Honey could you hold my pocketbook?"

I got into the conversation and told the cashier "make sure you don't let her go over five hundred, alright."

"I'll make sure you don't go over that amount", the cashier assured.

The cashier started ringing up the groceries. As she was ringing the groceries, I was putting stuff in bags as fast as possible. Shae continued to ask the cashier questions.

"Is the cream style corn still on sale", she asked?

"Yes it is, the cashier replied. They're two for a dollar."

"How about the Scott's tissue, is that still on sale?"

Shae looked at me and asked "do you wanna get those things for me while she's ringing up this stuff?"

"Nah, I said, let's just get what we got. We'll come back some other time to get the rest."

"He don't like shopping", the cashier said with a smile on her face.

"No, he doesn't but he don't have a choice", Shae replied. "Honey would you bring the car to the front of the store for me?"

"Yeah alright", I replied.

I knew that was the signal for me to roll the groceries out the store and head for the car and wait for her. I rolled the cart past the security guard. He looked at me with a smile on his face and even said for me to have a nice day. I took that as a sign. I put all the groceries in the back of the Jeep and waited for Shae to come out.

Not long after, she came walking out the store. When she got in, she gave me a kiss on the cheek and said, let's go. I was surprised at how easy that was. We pulled over to see how much groceries we had. It came out to five hundred twenty dollars.

"That went real smooth, Shae commented. We work well together, don't you think?"

"Yeah we do. Who we gonna sell this stuff to", I asked?

"I know a lot of people that have kids, Shae explained, they always looking for a deal. Drive back to Laurelton. I'll tell you where to go from there."

Before we got off the expressway, Shae took some of the meats out of the bags and changed the prices on them with a black pen. We drove up to 135th Avenue to this lady's house named Miss Keys. She was sitting on the front steps of her house watching her five kids playing in the front yard.

Shae and I got out the Jeep and walked over to the gate.

"Hey Miss Keys", Shae greeted.

"Hi baby. What you got for me today?"

"I got just what you need Miss Keys", Shae replied confidently.

"Yeah, how much it's gonna cost me?"

"That depends on how much you need."

"What you got", Miss Keys asked?

I walked to the back of the Jeep and pulled out the groceries and placed them on the steps next to Shae. Shae and Miss Keys went through the bags and Miss Keys said she'll take it all.

"How much you want for all this child?"

"The total, Shae explained, came up to seven hundred thirty dollars and some change. Gimme half for everything."

Miss Keys looked at the groceries and shook her head in agreement with the price Shae gave her. She reached in her bra to pull out a wade of cash and counted off four crisp hundred-dollar bills.

"Here baby, Miss Keys said. Count it to make sure it's correct."

"I trust you Miss Keys. You need anything else from the store?"

"Bring me whatever you got, she ordered, you know my check comes tomorrow. I'll be able to get more from you if you got it."

"Is there anything in particular you want me to get," Shae questioned?

"Steaks, Pork Chops, Chicken. Any kind of meat you can get your hands on", Miss Keys instructed.

"Alright, Shae confirmed, I'll see you tomorrow. Thanks."

As we walked to the Jeep, Miss Keys directed all her kids to grab the bags and carry them into the house. Shae and I got in the Jeep and pulled off. We drove through my block and went past my house. I didn't see anybody around and decided I'll stop to check out the damage the cops caused. In the front window of the house was a card from one of the detectives of the Tactical Narcotics Task Force with instructions for me to call him as soon as possible. I crumbled it up and threw it on the side of the house. The living room was a mess. They tore the cushions off the couch, turned over plants and tracked dirt throughout. In the sink in the kitchen, I saw where they poured out the contents of oatmeal containers hoping to find whatever stash they thought might be there. I was very careful not to stash drugs in my house. I always kept the drugs in the safe at the barbershop. First rule I learned a long time ago is to never shit where you live. That's the main reason I never kept drugs in the house. The cops even searched the sixty-gallon fish tank in the living room.

I could tell cause, all the rocks in the tank were pushed to one side. I didn't bother to look upstairs cause, I was sure they did a number up there as well. I stood in the living room before I walked out the door and shook my head in disbelief at how a house once filled with hope and promise now looked like a nightmare. I knew at that moment I could no longer live there. I walked outside to my Jeep.

"Is everything alright", Shae asked?

"It will be, I replied, as soon as we take a hit."

"Alright, Shae agreed, drive up Merrick to 228th Street and let's get this party started."

I didn't think of it as a party but more like an opportunity to escape from reality. I had to face the fact that everything I had was gone; my girl, my boys, the stores, the money; all gone. Slowly, I was even losing myself, and I knew it. Deep down I knew the way I was going would lead me nowhere. But for now, I didn't care. As long as I had my drugs, I'd deal with whatever later. We got back to the abandoned house, Shae and I sat on the couch and prepared ourselves to take a hit. She pulled out her antenna and I pulled out my brass pipe. I looked over at her and thought to myself, what a picture, from drug dealer to drug user. I thought if I took a hit, the thoughts I was having would fade away. But they didn't. In fact, thoughts flooded my brain. I thought all kinds of things. I thought about my moms and how brokenhearted she must be, *again*. I even thought about the chick Chase and I put in the back of his trunk. I never found out what happened to her. I could almost imagine. Casandra came to mind. All the time she put into our relationship and the hope she had we would be together. I caused that to be lost and now I had to deal with those feelings.

I felt hopeless and alone. The only thing I could rely on was the crack I was smoking. At times, that didn't even work.

"What's the matter", Shae asked?

"Ain't nothin'," I replied.

"Stop lying, Shae said, I can tell something's wrong Niko by the look on your face. You look like you're deep in thought. Tell me what you're thinking."

"I got a lot on my mind right now, I explained, and it looks like it's gonna get worst before it gets better."

"You thinking about your lady", Shae asked?

"That, along with a whole lot of other shit," I replied

"Niko, I know you may not want to hear this, but I know how you feel right now. All I can tell you is, things will work out. I've been through the same things you're going through right now. I lost my house, my job, and my husband. It seemed like everything just fell apart all at once. And just like you, the only thing I could do was numb my feelings by getting high. For a while it helped. But when the drugs wore off, I felt all that shit come crashing down on me all over again. You just gotta be strong and don't allow this situation to overwhelm you and have you making more bad decisions. You might, Shae continued, want to call on the Lord for some help."

"What you talkin' about? He ain't never helped me before. What he gonna do for me now", I asked? "You'd be surprised, Shae said with a smile on her face. Don't you know that God looks out for fools and babies? And as far as I can tell, we ain't babies no more. Just try it Niko. Trust him and see what he'll do for you", she concluded.

I thought to myself, how can this crack head bitch tell me what to do when she can't stop smokin' her damn self. She's telling me that God will make a way. So what happened to her? Don't he know she needs him too? Why should I believe that God cares about me?

"I know you don't believe what I'm saying Niko, I can see it on your face. But the truth is, we all go through shit one way or another. It just happens to be your turn."

Two For Five

"I hear what you sayin', I just don't buy into the idea that some blond haired, blue eyed mystery God is gonna come down off his *mighty* hill and save a nigga like me. That shit's for suckers. And I ain't one of them. And besides, if God looked out for fools, what happened to you?"

I could tell she was offended by what I said. She got up, put her antenna away and asked me to split the drugs we got so she could leave.

"I'm sorry Shae, don't leave. I hear you loud and clear. I've never had to look to anyone but my boys for help. Now that they're gone, I don't know how to handle this shit. know first and foremost, I need to face whatever it is I gotta face and get that shit over with. But, until I feel I can't run no more, I'm gonna smoke 'til I burn."

"You don't see Niko? You're burning now. I'm telling you, until you surrender yourself to God, things ain't gonna get any better, in fact, they gonna get worse. Take it from me."

"You sayin' all this stuff but you still smokin' crack. How I'm supposed to believe you," I asked? "Don't look at the messenger," Shae said, "hear the message. I know what God wants me to do. I just ain't ready to do it".

If I were you, I'd take a look at what God is trying to tell you. He took your partners away one by one and left you standing. Why Niko, why? He has a plan for you and you don't even know it. There's a scripture, Shae continued, in Job, Chapter Five, verse Seventeen that goes like this, "Consider yourself fortunate if God All

Powerful chooses to correct you. Remember that, Shae encouraged, cause that's what he's doing right now, correcting you."

Could she be right, I asked myself?

The next morning, Shae and I got up to go to another Key Foods to do our thing. We decided to go out on Long Island this time. As soon as we crossed over the borderline separating Queens from Long Island, we ran into a huge grocery store. We pulled into the parking lot and prepared to rob this place blind.

When we got inside, Shae said "don't rush. Take your time and shop like you got money." "Why don't we grab two shopping carts", I asked? "I'm down", Shae said boldly.

She and I rolled the carts through the sliding doors and again headed straight for the meat section. We filled the first cart with meats; Steak, Lamb Chops, Chicken, Pork Chops. You name it, we had it. We filled up the next cart with cereals, vegetables, and whatever else we could put our hands on. We looked for the cashier we thought would be talkative and not expect us to get over on her. We found one. She looked like she was in her late teens with a slender body. Her hair was pinned up in a bun. The nametag on her shirt indicated her name was Francine.

"Hi Francine", Shae greeted.

"Good morning ma'am."

"I need you to keep my total under seven hundred dollars", Shae instructed.

"Honey, could you hold my pocketbook? It's starting to feel kind of heavy around my neck." "Yeah babe, pass it to me", I replied.

"So Francine, how's life treating you", Shae asked?

"It's good, she replied. I just started here two days ago and I'm enjoying it."

"That's a good attitude to have, Shae commented. Where you from?"

"I don't live far from here."

Shae and the cashier continued to talk as she rang up the groceries. I listened while I stuffed the bags with groceries.

"Are you in school", Shae asked?

"Yes ma'am. I go to schools not to far from here."

"That's good, Shae complimented. Keep your head in them books, okay?"

I filled the first cart with the meats and started putting some of the other items from the second cart in the first one. I didn't wait for Shae to ask me to bring the Jeep around.

"I'm gonna bring the Jeep around to the front, alright?"

"Okay honey. Hurry up. She's almost finished ringing up the groceries."

I pushed the cart through the sliding doors and rolled the cart to the Jeep, opened the back door and threw the bags inside.

I got in, and watched Shae as she continued to talk to the cashier. She finished her conversation and started walking toward the door. Once she got outside, a security guard and some other guy grabbed her by the arm and led her back inside.

Damn, they got her. I sat there for a minute and continued to watch. The security guard and store manager were talking to her. I could see her waving her arms around in protest. The security guard and the store manager walked her out of my view. Five minutes passed and she still hadn't come out the store. I turned the ignition and drove slowly out the parking lot and parked across the street from the store. Ten minutes later, I saw a Nassau County Police car turn into the parking lot. I knew she was gonna be arrested but I waited to make sure. Ten more minutes passed and I saw the patrol car leave the parking lot. She wasn't in the back seat. What the hell's going on in there and why hasn't she come out yet? I was about to pull off when I saw her walk out from the parking area and stood in the middle of the block looking up and down the street. I blew my horn. She looked over to where the sound came from and smiled. When she got in, we looked at one another and just shook our heads.

"What happened in there", I asked?

"I was getting ready to walk out the store, she explained, when the security guard called me. The security guard and the store manager said I couldn't leave the store without paying for the groceries. I explained to them my boyfriend had my pocketbook and I needed to get it. They walked with me through the parking lot to see if we could find you. I was hoping you pulled off. When they couldn't find you, they called the cops. The cops told the store manager they couldn't do anything cause, I wasn't the one that walked out the store with the groceries. In fact, Shae explained, the cops told them they didn't have the right to hold me because they didn't catch me taking anything out the store. After the cops explained that to the store manager, the store manager told me not to come back to his store.

I looked at him as if to say, you definitely don't have to worry about that. When I saw that Jeep parked across the street, I knew I was alright. See, I told you, Shae concluded, just take it slow and everything will work out fine."

Chapter Seventeen

For the next few weeks, Shae and I continued to do our thing in the stores. Every Key Food we found, we robbed. If I had to put a dollar amount on the food we took, I would say it was in the thousands of dollars. Funny thing about it was how easy it was to rob them. Shae came up with *another* idea to get money out the department stores like J.C. Penny, Macy's, and Bloomingdales. She explained to me we need to find a person's account information and make up some I.D. to show *we're* that person. When we get to the department store, we'll go to the customer service department, she explained, and tell them we lost our charge card and would like to pay the balance due if they were able to give us a temporary card to shop. The only place to find customer account information is in mailboxes. Lefrak

Two For Five

City was the best place to find whatever we needed. With the number of buildings in that complex, we couldn't miss. Around one in the morning we drove over to Lefrak City to pop some mailboxes. Each building has three separate wings with three separate mailbox areas. We popped every mailbox we could. Instead of searching through the information we found right there on the spot, we put all the mail in a bag and carried it with us back to Laurelton.

Shae and I had plenty of drugs, and enough money to buy more if we ran out. That made it easy for us to concentrate on finding the right account to fuck with. We found ten good accounts. One account had thirty-five hundred dollars worth of available credit and the balance due was only two hundred dollars. In addition to finding the person's Bloomingdale account, we also found a box of blank checks with the person's name, address and telephone number on the top. When Shae saw *that*, she said the rest was easy.

The next morning we got up and put on our best outfits to go into Bloomingdales. We had to look the part if this was to work. I never really looked at Shae the way I did this morning. Shae stood about five feet five with an Anita Baker type haircut. Her complexion was a beautiful shade of brown with no blemishes. Shae always wore baggie clothes to hide the shape of her body. While she changed into the outfit she was gonna wear, I noticed how shapely and tone her body was. She had no stretch marks nor did her belly hang over the elastic band of her panties. She felt real comfortable undressing in front of me and I enjoyed every minute of it.

"Did you see all you need to see", Shae asked?

"What you talkin' bout girl? I wasn't paying you no mind," I replied.

"Liar! I saw you watching me," Shae said with a smile. "Maybe when we come back I'll show you some more."

I could tell she and I were getting close. The only reason I hadn't made a move on her is because all we were interested in was getting high. As time went on I found out Shae and I shared a common bond. We both had been hurt by past romantic situations and both of us chose to use drugs as a means to deal with the emotional scars.

"We need to stop by a stationery store," Shae said as she continued to change.

"For what," I asked?

"I need to get some supplies to make up the I.D."

When she finished dressing, she looked like someone I would definitely take notice of. She wore a pair of dark blue dress slacks with a low cut beige blouse and toeless pumps that exposed her beautifully polished toenails.

Before we walked out the house, she emptied her purse on the couch. All kinds of stuff was in there. She had pieces of balled up paper towel, torn up lottery slips, a change purse with no change in it, a nail file, an assortment of candies, and a wallet. When she found the *wallet*, it brought a smile to her face.

"Why you smiling," I asked?

"What's in here, she explained, is what I'm gonna use to make the I.D. we need."

Shae opened the wallet and showed me some passport size snapshots of herself.

"What they for, I asked?

"These, Shae explained, are the pictures for the I.D. that *you're* gonna help me make."

"I don't know how to make no damn I.D." I replied.

"You will by the time I'm finished with you." Shae transformed into a different person. The look in her eyes when it came to getting money, excited her. "You like this shit, don't you" I asked?

"Hell yeah," Shae replied. I get off on going into a store with no money and coming out of there with three, four thousand dollars worth of *free* stuff. You see Niko, Shae explained, it's not what you do, it's who you do it to. The trick I've learned, is to never give a person the opportunity to know they're being robbed. This way, when you walk away and they have a chance to think about it, they're too ashamed to let anybody know that somebody got 'em."

We picked up the items we needed from the stationery store and continued to make our way toward the Island. We pulled up in the parking lot of Bloomingdales at Roosevelt Field. The parking lot was packed. Shae took two blank checks out of the box of checks she had, put one of the checks in an envelope with the Bloomingdale statement along with the I.D. she made. The I.D. came out perfect. We walked into the store and picked up a store circular. The line in the customer service department wasn't long. In fact, we were next in line. Shae walked up to the counter and greeted the customer service representative.

"Good morning, Shae said with a smile. I need your help in solving a small problem."

"Yes ma'am, how can I help you," the representative asked?

"I seem to have lost my charge card somewhere and I knew you guys were having an excellent sale today. I was wondering if I paid the balance due would you be able to issue me a temporary card?"

The representative asked, "do you have your account number?"

"Yes I do, Shae said confidently. I have a statement of my account. Would that help?"

"Of course, ma'am. Just give me a second to pull up your account."

She pulled up the information on the computer and asked a series of questions to verify the account. "Are you Cynthia McKnight?"

"Yes I am", Shae said.

"And could you give me your current address?"

"9711 Horace Harding Expressway, Apartment 8-O," Shae replied.

"And ma'am, would you like to pay the balance due today?"

"Yes I would," Shae continued.

"And how much will you be paying?"

"The whole balance."

"How will you be paying", the representative asked?

"By check," Shae replied.

Shae filled out the check as they were talking and passed it to the representative.

"Miss McKnight, you said you lost your charge card and would like me to issue you a temporary one so you can shop today. Is that correct?"

"Yes it is," Shae replied.

"Ma'am, I can issue you another card but, the representative explained, I would have to charge your account for the extra card. Would that be alright?"

"Of course," Shae agreed.

"Then ma'am, all I'll need is your signature to compare to the signature we have on file and I'll issue you a temporary card.

Shae looked at me and smiled as if to say, we got this. She signed a piece of paper and the representative compared it to the signature she had on file. It must've been somewhat close to what the *real* customer's signature looked like.

The representative asked Shae, "How much credit would you like today?"

"As much as you can extend me," Shae commented.

"Okay ma'am, I'll give you fifteen hundred dollars to shop with today and as soon as your new card arrives, please put it somewhere safe."

"I'll remember that," Shae concluded.

The representative passed her the temporary card and told us, thank you for choosing Bloomingdales and have a nice day.

"Thank you for all your help, Shae replied, and you have a blessed day as well."

We walked away from the customer service area with smiles on our faces. As we browsed through the store, we passed a restaurant. Shae said she was hungry and asked if I wanted something to eat.

"Yeah alright," I confirmed.

We stepped inside the restaurant and sat down. A slim black chick, who looked to be no more than eighteen, came to our table and introduced herself.

"Good morning, the waitress greeted. My name is Carla and I'll be your hostess this morning. What would you like to order?

Shae and I looked at each other and just laughed.

"Good morning Carla, Shae greeting. What's good on the menu this morning?"

"We're currently serving brunch and the Chef has prepared an excellent dish I absolutely recommend."

"And what's that, I asked?

"It's a Spanish omelet topped with a spicy pico de gallo sauce. The omelet comes with two spicy chorizo sausage and a croissant.

"Okay, Shae agreed, we'll have two orders along with two tall glasses of orange juice."

"Will that be all ma'am", the waitress asked?

"Yes,' Shae replied.

Two For Five

Once the waitress took our order, Shae and I joked at how easy this shit was and how helpful people were being to assist us in milking this account.

Ten minutes passed and the waitress came back to our table with the orange juice and told us that our order should be ready momentarily. Shae and I both took sips of our juice and discussed what we were going to come out the store with. We both agreed we needed clothes for ourselves but, most importantly, we needed to get some things we could sell in order to keep money in our pockets. Shae explained, because the weather's about to change, we should concentrate on getting winter gear like coats, sweaters, and boots. After we finished eating our brunch, we toured the store looking for items we liked. We came across a new style of Timberland boots that Shae, nor I, had seen before. It fascinated me at how the stores out on the Island would have the latest fashions before any place else. Shae explained, that's the way it goes when it comes to fashion. Big companies put their newest product lines out to the big name stores to see if they'll sell and once they see that they will, they put it out to the smaller retailers. At least that's what Shae believed. We brought two pair of Tims and a couple of matching sweatshirts. That came up to four hundred dollars and some change. We moved on to the next area. As we walked through the store, I saw a bad ass Ralph Lauren sweater I knew would look nice on me. Shae saw I was interested in it and asked me if that's what I wanted. Of course, you know I said yes. She picked up the sweater and took it to the cashier.

"I'd like to get this for my man", Shae told the cashier.

The cashier looked at me with a smile and said, "Your wife has good taste."

"Yeah, I know", I replied.

The sweater cost a hundred and fifty dollars. We got three of them. Two of them, we would sell. I asked myself, who has that kind of money to buy these kinds of items? Then it hit me. Look at the area we're in. People out here on the Island have big houses and make the kind of money to afford the finer things in life. Shae and I passed by the jewelry section. She noticed a nice ring she was interested in getting for herself. We walked up to the counter and asked the cashier to show her the ring. She liked it. She asked the cashier if she could charge it to her account. The cashier proceeded to ring up the purchase. The cashier was taking a long time to process the order and Shae decided to ask her if there was a problem. The cashier said there was a hold on the account and that we needed to go to the customer service area to straighten it out. Shae asked if she could have her card back and that we would find out what was the problem. When we left from the jewelry area, I noticed that this guy was following us. He played it off like he was shopping but I could tell he wasn't. The first thing that drew my attention, was the fact that everywhere we went, he was there and he didn't have any items in his hands. I asked myself, who's gonna come to a department store, and not pick up one or two items? I pulled Shae's coat and told her we need to get outta there and take what we got and go on home. She said I was just paranoid and that it wouldn't look right if we just left the store like that. I kept telling her I didn't feel comfortable anymore and wanted to head for the exit. She finally agreed and we made our way towards the exits. As we approached the exit, a tall white guy with a security jacket on grabbed us by the arm and asked us to come with him. Behind us were two other tall white boys with walkie-talkies in their hands.

They escorted us to a back area where they took the items we purchased and asked us a number of questions. While one of them questioned us, the others were pulling the items we purchased out the bags and placing them on a table that sat in the corner of the room we were in. Above the table were a number of pictures of people that had been caught in the store for shoplifting. The security officers explained to us how they caught on to us. They told us the persons whose account we were using, had tried to make a purchase at another branch, and was told they couldn't shop because someone had been using their credit card. The person, they explained showed them her I.D. and confirmed that she was truly Cynthia McKnight. Then they told us they were waiting for the police to arrive to arrest us on charges of identity theft, grand larceny, and possession of stolen merchandise. My heart sank when he said that. Shae on the other hand, screamed on the security officers and told them they didn't have a case because we didn't walk out the store with the items. They quickly explained to her, as long as we used the card with the intent to defraud, they had a strong case. Not long after our conversation with the security officers, the police arrived. They took the merchandise we had purchased and handcuffed us both. We got to the precinct and were separated. The detective that interviewed me marveled at how smooth we operated up until we got caught. He asked me how we came up with a scam like that. I didn't say a word. He then asked me how I knew Shae. I lied and told him I've known her for a little over a year. He told me this isn't Shae's first time in that particular precinct and that she was arrested for the same thing two years ago. He told me he was impressed with how she pulled off her fraudulent scam and complimented her on how slick she was.

"The one thing that really gets to me, the detective stated, was having to lock up a seemingly intelligent person."

He went on to say that in all the years he's been a detective he's seen a lot of sheisty crooks. But Shae, in his opinion, was the best that ever did it.

Chapter Eighteen

Two days had passed and I still hadn't been to court. I found out that Nassau County has their own set of rules when it comes to producing their inmates before a judge. I tried numerous times to reach out to my attorney but didn't have any success. I even tried calling Casandra but she didn't answer her phone. Around three in the afternoon, a slender black Corrections Officer called my name. He said I had a visit and that I should stand by the door and wait for him to come back to pick me up. When he came back, he had six other inmates with him who were going on visits as well. We walked up a long hallway and through a series of electronic gates. At each point, the Corrections Officer said we were to remain quiet and stay to the left of the hallway.

Ahead of us were a group of inmates who were cleaning the facility. The difference between us and them was the way they were dressed. I had on this bright orange jumpsuit that had "Property of Nassau County" written on the back. They were dressed in dark green jumpsuits. We came to another set of electronic gates and were ordered by a nasty looking white officer to yell out our names so he could check to make sure we were supposed to be on a visit. He called off the first name. Manny Garcia, the C.O.

yelled. A voice from the rear of the group yelled, here. Gino Garvin. Again, a voice yelled out, here. Niko Bonds. Right here I replied. The officer looked at me and said, all I asked you to say was "here". Don't try to get smart *now* youngster, the officer said sarcastically. He continued to read off names until he called out the entire list. We walked through a metal detector and were directed to a room where we were searched. Once we all were searched, the officer directed us to another room where another set of officers stood.

There were six officers standing there looking at us in a way that if we blinked wrong they would take our heads off with a swing of their nightsticks. Niko Bonds, step up. I stepped out of line and walked towards the officer. Your visitor will be sitting at table nine. I walked through the visiting area and came to table nine, but no one was there. I looked around and didn't see anybody I recognized. To the left of me, a door swung open slowly and my moms walked through. I held my head down in shame. My moms walked over to the table and sat down and shook her head. "Hi baby, my moms said in a calm voice. How you doin?"

"Alright", I replied.

"You know you're killing me Niko, don't you? You think I like comin' to these places visiting you like some damn animal? What the hell you doin' to yourself? You don't even look like the Niko I know. What the hell's goin' on with you?"

I was about to open my mouth and say something when my moms said, "Don't you say a damn word. Just sit there and listen. I don't know what to do anymore. It's like you lost your damn mind or somethin'.

I looked down at the table and my moms slapped me across the side of my head and said, "Pay attention to me boy when I'm talking to you. Again, I tried to say something and my moms raised her hand and said, "I'll slap the hell outta you if you *dare* open your mouth."

"I've tried everything I could to get you to do the right thing Niko. And all you keep doing is messin' up. I found out the other day that your two partners, Clarence and Harvel, were murdered. Is that what's been botherin' you?"

I didn't know if I should answer her or not.

"You don't hear me talking to you boy? You better answer me when I'm talkin' to you child. I don't know if you know it or not, my moms explained, but Clarence's mother seems to think you had something to do with her son being murdered. Is that true Niko?"

I shook my head in disagreement.

"Then tell me what the hell happened?"

"Ma, I'm gonna tell you the truth, but I want you to know off the bat, I didn't have anything to do with Chase, I mean Clarence getting shot." Tears formed in my eyes for the first time in a long while and my moms just reached across the table and told me, "Mama's here baby." I rested my head on her shoulder. An officer came by and tapped my chair and told me I had to sit back or my visit would be cut short.

"Do you want people tellin' you for the rest of your life when you can go home?"

I didn't answer her. I just stared at her with tears rolling down my face. I could see some of the other inmates looking over at my moms and me. As soon as our eyes met, they would turn their heads.

I heard one of the C.O.s yell out, "You have five minutes to say your good byes."

My moms looked at me and said, "All I can do is pray for you Niko. I don't know what else I can do. You know it rips my heart out to see you back in this place. I'm gonna see if a friend of mine, who's a lawyer, can come to see you sometime this week. And if he tells me he can help you, whatever money I got Niko, I'll use it to help you out. You hear me baby?"

"Yes mama", I replied.

My moms got up from the table and squeezed me for dear life. Before she turned away, she looked me in my eyes and said, now it's time for you to ask for some help on your own.

I was told by the C.O. to sit down at the table until my visit had left the room. Once my moms left, I was escorted back into the room I was searched in. I was told to strip and turn around to spread my ass cheeks. After the search was over, the officer led me into another room to process the package my moms had left. She brought me some cosmetics, pictures, a bible, and put forty dollars in my account. I opened the bible. On the inside cover it read, "Acknowledge the Lord in all thy ways and he will direct your paths." That statement sent chills through my body. I knew right then that whatever was gonna happen, all I could do was handle it.

Again I was led through the long hallways and back to the dorm I was housed in. My Bunkie, an older guy in his late fifties, was standing by the beds he and I shared. He asked me how my visit was and I told him my moms came up to see me.

"Ain't nothin' like good old moms", he said.

"You got that right", I replied.

"So, young buck, what you in here for," he asked? "'I got caught in Bloomingdales out at Roosevelt Field doing some credit card shit."

"You like fuckin' with that plastic, he asked?"

"Yeah, it ain't bad until you get caught", I replied.

"Listen, my name is Covington. But you can call me Mister Fred. If you need anything, just let me know."

"Yeah, alright."

The nights were the hardest for me. I kept tossing and turning because the mattress was so lumpy. More than anything else was the blazing heat. The only one that was cool was the correction officer who had a fan in the bubble they sat in. Around two in the morning, my

Bunkie got up to go to the bathroom. When he came back he asked me why I wasn't sleep.

"I can't take the heat, I answered.

"Then you need to keep your young ass out the fire, he replied. "Listen, he continued, come with me in the bathroom."

I followed him into the bathroom and he pulled out a half a joint from under his dew rag.

"Here, take a couple of puffs off that. That'll help you sleep", he explained.

"What I gotta pay you for this", I asked?

"What you think, this some kind of homo shit? Nuh man, you ain't gotta gimme shit. Just take your ass to sleep and stop all that fuckin' movin' around, he concluded.

"Thanks man, but what about the smell?"

"Don't worry about the boys, he explained, they don't bother to come out that bubble after lights out. They too afraid one of us crazy niggas gonna string their ass up in here", he concluded.

I stood on the toilet seat and blew the smoke into the vent to kill the smell.

When I came out, Mister Fred asked, "You eat candy?"

"Yeah, I do, but ----Mister Fred interrupted me.

"Listen, I don't want nothin' from you. The way I was raised, if you got it, share it. This way the good Lord will always bless you. Now let's try this again. Your black ass want some candy?"

Two For Five

That was the first time I genuinely was able to smile since my boys passed. It got me to thinking about all the things I had been through and why the fuck I was still going through shit. The next morning I was awaken by the sounds of two officers yelling for everybody to get out of bed and stand for the count. Mister Fred leaned over toward me and said "That motherfucker there, ain't nobody to play with. He'll have your ass in the infirmary quicker than you can shake a stick. The other day, Mister Fred explained, there was this young kid that came through here. I wondered why I hadn't seen him after the first day. I found out, Mister Fred continued, that cracker had that young boy beat down for looking at him the wrong way. You ever been in the south, Mister Fred asked?"

"Nuh, I haven't", I replied.

"He is the complete, unabridged version of what the South is all about."

"Keepin' us niggas in line. He can't stand it when he sees a nigga come in here that likes to read or can talk real good. No sir, Mister Fred said with a deep Southern tone. He'll find reason to fuck with his ass. So boy, if you thinkin' about readin' anything' but that bible your mama brought you, think again."

After the count was over, all the inmates on the dorm were told to line up for chow. Everybody scrambled to get their cups so they could be the first in line to get coffee. Mister Fred took his time and when the coffee arrived he took our cups, walked straight to the front of the line and got some coffee. When he returned with the coffee, I asked him, how the fuck is it that an old man like you can skip past everybody and just bogard your way through.

"Cause I don't give a fuck, he explained. Niggas know who to fuck with in here. I don't bother nobody and damn sure ain't gonna let one of these so-called thugs, fuck with me. They better damn well recognize and leave me the fuck alone."

"What you in here for Mister Fred?"

"Well, that's a long story. I was about to leave work, he explained, to head home to the misses when I got a call from her. She asked me to pick up some bread and a couple of other things from the store. Now, I know my wife, he continued, in all the years I've known her, she's never called me to ask me to bring home shit but my tired ass. I got in my car and drove as fast as I could to my house. When I got there, I parked the car up the street and waited before I went in the house. About ten minutes after I parked the car, a guy came walking out *my house*. I drove the car in the driveway, like I do every night, and went inside. My wife was in the bathroom taking a shower. I looked in the kitchen to see if there was any bread, and found a whole loaf. When my wife came out the shower, I asked her if she knew there was bread on top of the refrigerator. She told me some bullshit about her not seeing it and forgot to call me to tell me not to bring any. The next day, I took off from work. My wife didn't know this. I backed the car out the driveway and drove up the street. I circled around the block and parked the car two houses away from mine.

Two For Five

An hour or so later, the guy I saw the other night comes boppin' up the street. I waited 'til he got in the house and gave them another ten minutes or so to do whatever they do. I walked in the house and didn't see them in the living room. So I went upstairs. They were in my bed fuckin' like it was alright.

When she looked up and saw me, she jumped outta bed and had this stupid ass look on her face. I still hadn't said anything and probably wouldn't have done anything until her asshole boyfriend said some slick ass shit. I opened the closet door, pulled out my revolver and shot that nigga right there on the spot."

"So you here for murdering your wife, I asked?"

"No, I'm here for killin' a nigga fuckin' my wife."

After he told me that, I left Mister Fred alone for a while. Around noon, one of the correction officers called me to the bubble. He told me my lawyer was in the visiting area and that I would be taken down to see him in a little while. The only lawyer I was expecting was Jonathan Goronsky. But it wasn't him. It was the lawyer my moms told me she would get in contact with. We sat down at the table and talked about my case. He told me that the Queens Narcotics Task Force already knew where I was along with my Parole Officer, and that they were in the process of having me brought back to Queens County to face the charges there. He went on to explain that the case over in Queens was a lot more serious than the case in Nassau. The charges Queens had on me were so numerous that my attorney told them he would talk to me about copping out to all charges in exchange for leniency. He told me the process was already in effect and that I should be transferred by that afternoon. I wasn't looking forward to going through this shit but I knew I had to in order to get this taken care of.

The first person I ran into when I got to Queens Criminal Court was my P.O. She looked me up and down like she did the first time I met her.

"You know Mister Bonds, you really piss me off. I knew all the while something was up with you. Now look at you.

All fucked up again. Do you know that you're facing seven and a half to fifteen years in jail?" Do you also know that if it wasn't for your mother, I would recommend the court give you the maximum sentence? But, I came up with an idea that you *really* need to consider. I've been speaking with your attorney who's under the impression that you're not a bad kid and may need a break. We decided to present you before the judge and see if we could get you into a special training program for parole violators."

"What kinda program", I asked?

First, a substance abuse counselor will interview you. Based on their recommendations to the court, you'll be allowed to get into a program. Once you've been accepted, my P.O. explained, you'll be transported to a facility for ninety-seven days. You'll have to complete the *entire* program in order to keep from going to jail. The program is called Willart. It's an intense boot camp style training course that will get you used to taking orders and respecting authority figures. After you complete

Willart, you'll be assigned to an in-patient treatment facility for a period no less than eighteen months. Are you with me so far Mister Bonds, my P.O. asked?"

"Yeah, I hear you."

"You don't seem too happy with the idea."

"It's not that, I explained, I never been in anything like that before. So I don't know what to expect. You tellin' me all this shit about *boot camp*. What the fuck's all that about", I asked?

"If you don't take the program, Mister Bonds, your ass is going back upstate. Without a doubt", my parole officer concluded.

"So, if I don't complete the program, then what happens?"

"You'll have to do the seven and a half to fifteen."

"That's a fucked up deal you're offering me. On the one hand, you're telling me if I don't take the program, I'm gonna be sentenced to seven and a half to fifteen, and if I don't complete the program, I'll still get the same time. What kinda shit you trying to pull," I asked?

"Mister Bonds, you don't have to take the program at all. You can go upstate and do the time, my P.O. explained, or you might want to start changing some of the behaviors that keep you in and out of jail. You decide," she concluded.

Chapter Nineteen

After I talked with my P.O. and attorney, I was taken to a processing area in the Queens House of Detention. A correction officer told me tomorrow I would go before the judge. In addition to having to appear in court, I would have to go through a parole revocation hearing to determine if parole would go along with the recommendation of the court or place me in a treatment facility or have me serve my time in a state prison. As I was being processed, I listened to some of the other parole violators' talk about the program I was about to get into. The shit I heard them say they had to go through had me thinking I was better off doing the bid. I overheard one guy say the instructors are always in your face yelling at you and degrading you. I don't think

I could go for that without punching one of them ma'fuckers in the mouth.

"Bonds, a correction officer yelled, step up!"

I approached the officer and was told to stand behind a yellow line.

"Time to take your picture", the officer said.

I stood with my back against the wall. The officer snapped my picture and told me to pick up a tray of food and have a seat in cell number three. Inside the cell were two guys having a conversation about the Willart program. I heard one of them say if you don't follow a drill instructors order, they made you do a lot of physical shit like running around the entire complex, or crawling on your belly until the drill instructor tells you to stop. As the conversation continued, the shit I was hearing had me fucked up. I ain't gonna make it through that shit, I thought. I know me. I'd fuck around and smash one of them ma'fuckers real quick. I interrupted their conversation to get some more information.

"Pardon me brother, can I ask you something about that Willart shit you talkin' about?"

"Go ahead", the guy replied.

"My P.O. told me about the program y'all talkin' about. What's up with it?"

"What you wanna know?"

"What's it like?"

"You ever been in the Army?"

"Nuh."

"Brother, you in for a ride."

"Why you say that", I asked?

"Them drill instructors don't fuckin' play. They'll have your ass beggin' to do the state time. I should know, I just flunked out."

"How much time you facing", I asked?

"Three to nine", the brother replied.

"Bonds, let's go, an officer yelled! You're going upstairs to your floor."

Me and ten other guys got on an elevator and rode to the floors we were to be assigned to. I was on the sixth floor. When I stepped off the elevator, another officer told me to stand against the wall and wait for my name to be called and someone would show me to my cell. The floor I was on was for parole violators. I heard my name called and followed a short balding officer to my cell. As I walked through the tier, I couldn't help but notice how small the cells were. If I stretched my arms, I could touch either side of the cell. I was escorted to cell twenty-one all the way in the back of the tier. The toilet inside the cell didn't have a toilet seat and was made of steel. Some cold shit to sit on. The sink didn't have a faucet to turn the water on.

I would have to push a button for the water to come out and hold it down to keep the water running. On the walls were little sayings that people before me wrote. One of the sayings made me think. It read: In this cell I wait. Tomorrow in court I find out my fate. I know I face many years. But that can never compare to all my tears. From today forward I have to remain cold. In order for me to do this time I must hold. So here I sit in this darken place. Not a man, not a son, just another case.

Two For Five

After I read it, I sat down on my bed and thought about all the things that happened up to this point. I lost two of my best friends in less than a year. If I hadn't been out there selling drugs, maybe they'd still be here. My lady Casandra, I miss the hell outta her. I fucked up on that as well, and now all I can do is think about the mistakes I made. Damn, my moms. I know she's the main one that's hurting right now. I hope she can forgive me for all the pain I caused. For now, I can't think about that. I gotta do me. I pulled out the bible my moms had brought me and began to read a few verses. Around four thirty in the afternoon, one of the officers came to my cell and told me I had to meet with a parole counselor. The officer took me to the tenth floor and told me to have a seat by an office that had two officers inside. When the officers saw me, they told me to come inside and have a seat. I sat in front of the officers and waited for him to say something.

"Your name", the officer asked?

"Niko Bonds", I replied.

"Your parole officer asked us to process you through for the Willart program. You aware of that"?

"Yeah, she mentioned it to me earlier."

"Are you willing to go through the training they provide?"

"I guess so. I really don't have a choice."

"You got a choice." You can either go into the program or handle your business and do the time. Whatever you decide, you need to face your drug problem."

"I don't have a drug problem", I replied.

"Yes you do. Otherwise you wouldn't be here talking to me", the officer said.

"All I did was smoke a little crack, I explained. But that didn't have me fucked up to the point I couldn't take care of myself."

"It don't have to have you fucked up, the officer explained. If you take a look at the things that have been happening in your life that caused you to get locked up, and have to talk to someone like me, then getting high has taken control of your life. I hate to tell you this young blood, I've seen a lot of characters like you come through here that thought they didn't have a drug problem as well. A year later, I hear about them being back in jail, or in the morgue. You're being given a prime opportunity to get your life back in order. You can use this time to find your way out of the shit you got yourself into, the officer explained, or you can bullshit your way through and wind up right back in a place like this or worse. It's your choice".

I sat there and thought about the choices I had and decided that doing time is something I'm familiar with. I've never had to take responsibility for my self or worry about the direction of my life.

"Let me tell you about the program, "the officer continued. The program is a little over three months long and involves some very intense training. For the most part, the program will help you determine how bad you want to change your life."

"The drill instructors will grill you on a daily basis to help build character and teach you to follow delegations and directions. It's not an easy thing to go through, the officer explained. If you flunk the course, you'll be sent back to prison to serve your time. And, the officer explained, the time you spent in Willart won't count towards your jail time. If you're interested in getting into the program, I'll need you to sign some papers indicating that you agree to the terms set forth. Once you sign, the next part will be on the courts to accept our recommendation."

Once he finished explaining the program to me, I was taken back down to my floor. When I got there, dinner was being served. The food they served was franks and vegetarian beans. I hadn't eaten in days and tore right into it. I finished dinner and went back to my cell to lie down and get some rest. By the time I woke up it was five o'clock in the morning. A

C.O. was walking past my cell and told me I needed to get ready for court and that someone would be coming to pick me up in a little while to take me down to the holding cells.

Court didn't start 'til nine thirty. I couldn't understand why I had to get up so early to go right here in the building.

"Open up twenty-one, an officer yelled!" Bonds, step out. You have court today."

Two guys from the tier and myself were the only ones that had to be in court. We got downstairs and were told to have a seat in a small bullpen that sat by a door used to bring other inmates in. Every time the door opened, I could feel the cold morning air. Breakfast was served through the bars of the cell. We had cold coffee, and a cold egg sandwich.

One of the guys in the cell with me joked with the C.O. that we needed a microwave inside the cell. The C.O. responded by saying, "I guess that'll make you feel right at home, wouldn't it?"

Around nine a.m., the C.O.s started calling out names to be brought upstairs to court. I was among the first group. They moved us from one bullpen to another. Bullpen therapy, that's what they call it. When it was time for me to go before the judge, my attorney came to speak to me. He told me he spoke to the District Attorney and their office was going to argue against the possibility of me getting a program. They wanted me to do the jail time. All seven years of it. My attorney told me not to worry. He said the judge was a former schoolmate of his and he'll speak to him on my behalf. Two minutes later, a court officer came to get me. I walked in the courtroom and saw my mother sitting in the front row. Her face showed the hurt and pain she was going through, once again. She held a white handkerchief in her hand to wipe the tears from her eyes. Before I turned around to face the judge, Casandra walked through the door. That kinda threw me for a second. The court officer had to call my name twice to get me to face the judge. All the while the judge was talking to my attorney, I was thinking about how good Casandra looked walking through those doors. The thought of her being there touched the hell outta me. I turned around once again to see where she was. Casandra sat right next to my moms with her arm around her shoulder. Your honor, my attorney began, my client is ready to plead guilty to all charges against him. We ask the court to accept the recommendation of Mister Bonds' parole officer who suggested that Mister Bonds be allowed to go into an in-patient treatment facility to address his substance abuse issues.

Your honor, the district attorney interrupted, it's admirable that Mister Bonds wants to address his drug problem but, the state feels that given the defendant's recent release from prison less than a year ago, and his subsequent arrest on the current charges, indicates that the defendant has no regard for the stipulations of his parole. We feel that the defendant should be considered a threat to the public and locked away for the maximum allowable time period.

Let's not lose sight of an important fact, your honor, my attorney argued, Mister Bonds' parole officer felt it necessary that Mister Bonds be allowed to address his substance abuse issues and to pursue his treatment outside of a prison environment. I'm sure, my attorney continued, your honor is familiar with the boot camp training program called Willart. Mister Bonds has been interviewed by the counselors for that program and they've agreed to accept Mister Bonds in their program with the stipulations that he complete the program in the time allowed or be remanded back to the custody of the Department of Corrections to serve out his time.

The frail looking district attorney continued to express his objections so much so that the judge bound the case over for a month to sort through the information.

"I'll need some time, the judge said, to determine if sending this defendant to an intense program will benefit him or if sending him to jail would serve the interest of society."

"Your honor, can I say something on my sons behalf?"

I turned around and saw my moms standing up from her seat to say something to the judge. "Yes Ms. Bonds, you can", the judge replied. "Your honor, my son has been in trouble with the law so much that I don't know what to do anymore to help him. His parole officer told me about this Willart program she wants him to get into and I understand that it's designed to help people like him learn self discipline. Niko needs this program or I'm afraid instead of me seeing him in prison greens, I'll have to buy him a black suit for his funeral. I can't stress enough the importance of this court deciding in favor of this young man's life and let my son get a real chance at living his life like a normal human being should. Please your honor, don't send my son away again but put him through the ringer if necessary to shake his brain up and get him to change his ways from the path of destruction he's on, to the path that leads to life. If you have kids your honor, my moms continued, I know you know how difficult it is to raise a child, and even more difficult to raise that child alone as a single parent. I'm asking the court today, to hear a mother's request to have her son back and not lose him to the system.

Ms. Bonds, the judge began, I've seen a lot of youngsters come through my court over the years and never had the privilege to hear such heart wrenching sincerity as I hear here today. I will take into consideration your request and have a decision for you in one month. Please, Ms. Bonds, I ask you to trust in the system for once and allow me to make the appropriate choice regarding both your son and society at large.

The district attorney looked like he was about to bust after hearing the words the judge said. His face turned a bright red. I guess he was looking to send my ass away for as long as he possibly could, but not today.

The court officer led me away to the holding cells. Inside, my attorney came to speak to me. He told me he was going to meet with the district attorney later that day and discuss the possibility of me getting into the program. He also stated the judge sitting on the bench greeted him after I left out the court and he'd be speaking to him as well.

"Bonds, a C.O. yelled, on the go back. You ready to go up?"

"Yeah, let's get outta here", I replied.

As I rode the elevator with the C.O., he looked over at me and said, "you have a good chance of getting what you're asking for. I know cause, I had a chance to speak to the parole counselors last night and they feel you could benefit from their program.

"Then why, I asked, is the district attorney trying so hard to get me to do the jail time?"

Because that's their job, the C.O. stated. They're not going to give everybody a chance to get out of going to jail. They'll be out of a job. So sit tight young man and be easy. Don't worry so much about the things you can't change. During the time I was waiting for my court date to come up, I had a chance to reflect back on some of the things I couldn't see while I was in the midst of it. My mans and them, Ming and Chase, both gone. Who would've thought the day would come when I wouldn't be able to reach out to them. The thought of where the drug game had taken us made me realize life is too short to waste time fucking around with bullshit.

I came to the conclusion, that whatever I need to do to get my life back on track, I'd do; even if it meant having to do the jail time.

Lights out, I heard one of the C.O.s yell.

As the lights went out on the tier, I thought to myself, I'm back in this shit again. One of the C.O.s walked slowly across the catwalk. The heels of his shoes had a rhythm that helped me sleep. As I drifted off, I tried to remember how it felt to have my lady laying by my side cuddling next to me. For right now, I got to forget about that until that time comes.

Chapter Twenty

Two days before I was to appear in court, my attorney came to visit me. He told me the district attorney has been stalling the proceedings to see if they could come up with more charges. It's been six months since my case started. The presiding judge took to heart the statement my moms made and has been swaying towards the idea of putting me in a program. The district attorney's pissed off about that. They want me to do the jail time.

"That explains, my attorney said, why it's taking so long to close out this case. I need you to continue to be patient Mister Bonds, and let me work this out with the judge."

"How much longer do you think it's gonna take," I asked?

"I don't know, my attorney explained, but what I do know is sooner or later they're gonna have to give us a decision."

Over the last six months, Casandra's been coming to visit me. She brings me things I need like cosmetics, reading material, or whatever else I asked. But mostly she's been there to offer her support. Yesterday, when Casandra came to see me, she told me she broke it off with the guy she was seeing.

"Why'd you do that", I asked?

"I can't ignore how I feel about you, Niko. It's obvious I'm still in love with you. When he would touch me, she explained, I would think about you and how you used to touch me. Even when he and I had sex, I imagined it was you. Don't get me wrong, she continued, he's a nice person, but *no one* makes love to me the way you do."

Her words stuck in my head ever since. I know I hurt her beyond what any woman should accept. A lot of times, I wished she would've found someone who wouldn't treat her the way I did. She deserves to be happy. She and I talked about getting back together when all this was over. But for now, I was glad to have her as a friend. It's not easy mending broken fences. Especially, when someone you love has broken them. The day I was to go to court, a strange feeling came over me. I felt calm. Like whatever was gonna happen would be alright. A guy in the next cell from mine named Preach came in my cell and told me he prayed for me. I didn't know this guy from a hole in the wall but to hear him say he prayed for me, helped. When I stood before the judge the district attorney said they still hadn't completed their investigation and needed another adjournment to sort out their information.

"What kinda information are you pursuing counselor", the judge asked?

"Your honor, we found that Mister Bonds, and another defendant, were cohorts in a money making enterprise that involved Mister Bonds receiving stolen credit cards and using those cards to defraud stores of their merchandise. We're asking the court to allow us to continue our investigation in its entirety."

"How much *more time* do you need counselor", the impatient judge asked?

"Your honor, the district attorney's office can't put a time limit on pursuing justice and ask your honor to extend our adjournment for at least one more month."

"Counselor, the judge said in a commanding voice, you don't expect this court to allow you to go on a fishing expedition at the expense of the defendant's right to a speedy conclusion to this case, do you? If that's what you're looking to accomplish, think again counselor."

"Your honor, the state understands this case has taken a considerable amount of the court's time and we're asking the court to take into consideration the new information we're pursuing."

Finally, my attorney stood up and objected.

"Your honor, the defense has accommodated the district attorney's office in every possible way and feels that any further delay in concluding this case would be a great disservice to my client."

The district attorney paused for a minute to speak with one of her colleagues.

"Your honor, the state is prepared to forego any further investigation if the defendant pleads guilty to all charges. Furthermore, the state is willing to allow Mister Bonds the opportunity to pursue his treatment request, if he agrees to our stipulations."

"What kind of deal are you offering", my attorney questioned?

"The defendant would have to admit that he, along with his accomplice, did in fact defraud Macy's Department Store,

J.C. Pennys, and a number of other businesses, over the course of seven and a half months, for the purpose of personal financial and materialistic gain. Second, the defendant, and his accomplice, did know the credit cards they were using were stolen and that they ignored the letter of the law to pursue their felonious endeavors. Thirdly, the defendant, upon admitting these facts, will accept the maximum penalty under the law."

"You're asking my client to plead guilty to allegations that he took part in a credit card scheme. The only problem is, you have yet to produce any evidence to support your claims. How, my attorney argued, do you expect my client to agree to those terms?"

"Your honor, the district attorney complained, not being able to put all the pieces to this puzzle together is why we're asking the court to give us the time we need to prove our case."

The judge leaned back in his chair and folded his arms. He looked over at my attorney and me and spoke in a clear voice.

"I've made a decision. The district attorney's office has until the end of the week to come up with the evidence it needs to prove its case. If by that time, the judge concluded, you don't have the proof you need, I'll make my ruling."

Two court officers stepped along side of me and took hold of me. The judge set my next court date for the end of the week. He remanded me to lock up and told the district attorney to have her case together when she came back to court. The court officers escorted me out of the courtroom. As I walked out the courtroom, I saw Casandra and my moms sitting in the same front row seats they sat in since this case began. Casandra blew me a kiss and my moms motioned with her lips, "I love you."

While the court officer was taking off my handcuffs, he told me the judge was pissed off because the district attorney didn't have her case together and because of that, I might get the program I'm looking for.

"Bonds, another C.O. yelled, on the go back."

I got on the elevator and rode up to my floor. When I got off the elevator, Preach was standing at the gate.

"What happened", he asked?

"The district attorney tried to pin some more charges on me, I explained, but the judge wasn't going for it."

"I told you, Preach said, the Lord helps those that believe."

For the next few days, Preach and I spent a lot of time talking about our experiences. He told me he too was in the drug game and lost everything as well.

"What helped me, he explained, I learned to trust in the Lord. I knew what I was doing was wrong. Selling drugs to people who would beg, borrow and steal to get what they needed. The money and the lifestyle attracted me, that's why I couldn't stop. When I realized the effects the drugs I was selling had on people, I turned away from that life and decided to do as God commanded. That's why I told you the other day, I prayed for you. I see me in you young blood, and I want you to know you don't have to live like that no more. God can turn things around for you if you let him. The court thing you're going through right now is no coincidence. It's God's will. So whatever happens, know that God is making a way for you. All you got to do, preach concluded, is trust him."

Thursday morning arrived and so did my court date. Again, I sat in the bullpen wondering what would be my fate. My attorney came into the bullpen area to speak with me.

"I haven't heard any new information from the district attorney's office about new charges being brought against you. I guess they couldn't find anything.

Hopefully, the judge will let us know how he feels about you going into a program. Just hang tight, my attorney said, and I'll have them call you in a few minutes."

While I waited to be called, I thought about what Preach had told me about trusting in the Lord. I never asked anyone for help in my life. But now, I felt I needed to.

"Lord, I don't really know if you can hear me, but I'm gonna say what's on my mind. I know the way I've been living is not the way you intended. For that, I apologize. You know what I'm up against and I'm sure you know I'm gonna have to do some time. What I'm asking is that the district attorney has no new information to hold up this case any further. Please Lord, help me out, give a brother a break. I need to get myself together and if you feel it necessary for me to go into a program, then Lord make it happen. Oh, thanks for listening."

"Bonds step up", the court officer yelled.

I stood up and felt butterflies floating in my gut. I nervously walked through the courtroom doors. My moms and Casandra sat in their usual seats and waved at me as I entered the courtroom. In the back of the court, were two serious looking white boys in tightly pressed blue uniforms.

"Good morning, your honor", the district attorney greeted.

"Good morning counselors. Is the prosecution prepared to present the new evidence it has", the judged asked?

"Your honor, the district attorney's office has not completed it's investigation and would like the court to make its ruling."

"Do you have a problem with that defense counsel?"

"No your honor, my client is prepared for sentencing."

"Then let's get on with this, the judge said. In the matter of the State of New York verses Niko Bonds, I hereby accept the defendant's plea of guilty to three counts of conspiracy to sell and distribute a controlled substance, which carries a penalty of no less than seven and half years with a maximum of fifteen years.

With regard to defense Counsel's request to allow the defendant an opportunity to seek help for his substance abuse problem, the court finds the defendant is eligible. I hereby remand the defendant into the custody of the Willart program with the following stipulations. The defendant will comply and complete all program activities. Upon completion of the Willart program, the defendant will be placed in an in-patient drug treatment facility for six months. Upon completion of the in-patient program, the defendant will complete a six month outpatient program. After all phases of treatment have been complied with, the defendant will be placed on one year of intense parole supervision. If any of these stipulations have not been complied with, the defendant will be remanded into the custody of the Department of Corrections to serve a prison term of seven and a half years to fifteen years."

When the judge asked if there were representatives in the court from the Willart Program, the two serious-looking white guys stepped up.

"Yes your honor, we're from Willart and are prepared to accept custody of the defendant." The judge looked at me and said, "Mister Bonds, you're being given an opportunity that the court feels you need to take full advantage of, understand? I truly feel that if you do as you're told, you can turn your life around and lead the productive life your mother so graciously desires for you to enjoy. Don't waste this chance. This case is hereby closed. Bailiff, escort the defendant out of my courtroom", the judge concluded. When I got back to my cell, I packed my things and waited for the Willart instructors to pick me up. Preach showed me a few verses from the bible for encouragement. He said they would come in handy in times of hardship and trouble.

"You're gonna need these to get through the battle you're about to face", he explained.

"What you talkin' about?" You make it seem as through I'm going to fight a war."

"You are! You just don't know it yet. Let me explain what you're getting ready to face. The one person you haven't been able to figure out all your life is. YOU! You're gonna go through some things in order to find your path, Preach continued. It's not gonna be easy, but the Lord, who's directing you, is gonna turn your life around if you let him. Don't be afraid of what you come up against. Be open to the experience, and ask God to show you the truth," Preach said.

I didn't have a clue what he was talking about. To be honest, I thought he was acting a little weirder than normal. Nonetheless, I listened to him. It's because of him I started talking with this *God* person.

"Bonds, let's go", the C.O. yelled. You got people waiting for you."

Ten people, along with me, were scheduled to go into the Willart program. We all got on the elevator and were taken to the bullpen area to be handcuffed. Two of the Willart instructors walked into the bullpen to handcuff us one by one. We were directed to stand, single file, by the exit. After everyone was hooked up, another Willart instructor came in. He had a beige outfit on with a gold badge and wore his hat tilted towards the front. As soon as he stepped in the lock-up area, the other officers saluted him. He looked like he didn't take shit from anybody, including his team. By the way the officers stood at attention, I knew this was the top dog of this outfit.

"Good morning gentlemen. My name is Sergeant Russ Daniels. I'll be one of the instructors assigned to whip your asses back into line, with what society considers a productive member. I will not, he continued, stand for any bullshit from any of you whatsoever. If you feel you're ready to become men, I'm here to help you accomplish that. The Willart program is designed to develop character and to break you of the behaviors that have brought you to this point. You will address me, as well as my staff, in the appropriate manner at all times. NO EXCEPTIONS! When you hear your name called, you will respond by saying, SIR, YES SIR. Anything other than that will not be tolerated. Do I make myself perfectly clear?"

The entire group responded by saying "SIR, YES SIR", in loud, clear voices.

"That being said, Sergeant Daniels concluded, welcome to Willart."

About the Author

I'm a Self Published Author and Chief Executive Officer of Real Talk Media. A company dedicated to "bringing you the drama of the streets."

I have a degree in accounting and a PHD from the streets. I developed my writing skills as a means of identifying the areas in my life where I made some bad decisions. As a result, I discovered my life has been filled with nothing but drama.

Two for Five, which is the title of my first book, was written in fictional form based on my personal experiences hustling on the streets of New York and eventually becoming a user of the same drugs I sold. I struggled with my addiction for many years but could never achieve sobriety because I lacked a conscious contact with a power greater than myself.

I've completed an intense inpatient treatment program in Harlem where I addressed my numerous years of substance abuse to crack cocaine and continue to maintain my sobriety on a daily basis.

In addition, I've developed a personal relationship with God and truly believe had it not been for God's Grace and Mercy, I would still be trapped in the grips of my addiction. I wrote "Two for Five" not just for the purpose of entertaining but as a means of depicting the cycle of destruction that has devastated my life and continues to threaten many others in our communities.

It's my hope that the characters in my book will cause the reader to reflect on the course and direction of their life and make a decision to change or face the consequences of their choices.

To schedule a book signing,
please call: 646-837-2560

To comment about the book, please email me
at: lawrencedbrown245@yahoo.com

Real Talk Media

58 Evergreen Lane
Suite10D
Newark, NJ 07107

Order Form

Email: lawrencedbrown245@yahoo.com
Ebooks: https://www.createspace.com/4274969

Name: _____

Inmate ID# _____

Address: _____

City/State: _____ Zip:_____

QUANTITY	TITLES	EACH	TOTAL PRICE
_____	Two For Five	$15.00	$ _____
	…Coming Soon…		
_____	Two For Five 2	$15.00	$ _____
		Sub Total	$ _____
		Shipping	$ _____
		Total Enclosed	$ _____

Shipping and Handling: $4.95. Add $1.50 for each additional book.
Disclosure: Please send full retail price of $15.00 per book. All payments are to be submitted by Institutional check or money order, including shipping and handling cost, to the address above. Payment sent with insufficient funds will be returned.

Thank you.

Real Talk Media

58 Evergreen Lane
Suite10D
Newark, NJ 07107

Order Form

Email: lawrencedbrown245@yahoo.com
Ebooks: https://www.createspace.com/4274969

Name: _____

Inmate ID# _____

Address: _____

City/State: _____ **Zip:**_____

QUANTITY	TITLES	EACH	TOTAL PRICE
_____	Two For Five	$15.00	$ _____
	…Coming Soon…		
_____	Two For Five 2	$15.00	$ _____
		Sub Total	$ _____
		Shipping	$ _____
		Total Enclosed	$ _____

Shipping and Handling: $4.95. Add $1.50 for each additional book.
Disclosure: Please send full retail price of $15.00 per book. All payments are to be submitted by Institutional check or money order, including shipping and handling cost, to the address above. Payment sent with insufficient funds will be returned.

Thank you.

Made in the USA
Middletown, DE
29 December 2022

17734195R00141